The

CREATIVE MANAGER

ROGER EVANS PETER RUSSELL

UNWIN
PAPERBACKS

LONDON SYDNEY WELLINGTON

First published in Great Britain by the Trade Division of
Unwin Hyman Limited, 1989

First published in paperback by Unwin® Paperbacks, an imprint
of Unwin Hyman Limited, in 1990

UNWIN HYMAN LIMITED
15–17 Broadwick Street
London W1V 1FP

Allen & Unwin Australia Pty Ltd
8 Napier Street, North Sydney, NSW 2060, Australia

Allen & Unwin New Zealand Pty Ltd with the Port Nicholson Press
Compusales Building, 75 Ghuznee Street, Wellington, New Zealand

British Library Cataloguing in Publication Data

Evans, Roger, 1941–
   The Creative Manager.
1. Management. Creative thought.
I. Title   II. Russell, Peter, 1946–
658.4'03
ISBN 044406045

Printed in Great Britain by Cox & Wyman Ltd, Reading

The unprecedented pace of change facing us in the 1990s demands that we draw upon our creative resources as never before. *The Creative Manager* stands alone in its uniquely practical approach to stimulating creative thinking and problem solving. It explores what it really takes to be creative in the face of the complex new challenges facing businesses today.

Based on the authors' extensive consultancy and training work in major companies around the world, it is a handbook for the managers of tomorrow. Yet because the principles it deals with are common to each of us, it is relevant to everyone.

'Successful managers will be those who have the capability to learn and also to bring creative thinking to the problems they confront. I have found the outlines of this process contained in *The Creative Manager* both fascinating and useful. They codify and explain some of the thought processes that I and many others have been following unconsciously for years.

All of us have blatant creative ability and it behoves us to apply ourselves to improving this capacity in just the same way as any other aspect of our craft. *The Creative Manager* can, I believe, help this process.'

Sir John Harvey-Jones, MBE

'This is a radical book but I have a strong feeling that the ideas incorporated here will become mainstream within a few years. Reading it was like coming home.'

Anita Roddick, The Body Shop International Plc

'A sensational book on personal empowerment. The real revolution in the information age is the ability to use our minds differently. *The Creative Manager* will be your guide.'

John Sculley, CEO Apple Computers Inc.

'This is an exciting book, useful and uplifting, full of belief in the human potential for two people who obviously know what they are talking about.'

Prof. Charles Handy Visiting Professor, London Business School

'The authors have produced an imaginative and humanistic approach to one of the major concerns of the 1990s – how to manage the balance between the inner world of intuitions and the outer world of sense realities. Deserves to be read widely.'

Tudor Rickards Director, Creativity Unit, Manchester Business School

'This book is for everyone. The elements of creativity which Peter Russell and Roger Evans identify are common not only to business management but to the everyday challenge of living up to our fullest human potential. I recommend it.'

Marilyn Ferguson Author, *The Aquarian Conspiracy*

To
Joan and Anna
for their love and support

Life is moving far more rapidly now than ever before —
typically in the rate of growth of facts, knowledge, tech-
niques and inventions. We need a different kind of human
being, able to live in a world which changes perpetually,
who has been educated to be comfortable with change in
situations of which he has absolutely no forewarning. The
society which can turn out such people will survive; socie-
ties which do not will die.

Abraham Maslow (1976)

Only the individual can think, and thereby create new
values for society, nay, even set up new moral standards to
which the life of the community conforms. Without creative
personalities able to think and judge independently, the
upward development of society is as unthinkable as the
development of the individual personality without the
nourishing soil of the community.

The health of society thus depends quite as much on the
independence of the individuals composing it as on their
close social cohesion.

Albert Einstein (1955)

CONTENTS

ACKNOWLEDGEMENTS

With a book of this nature, based on our experience with a number of organizations and people, there are many individuals whom we would like to thank. Without the support of Rose-Marie Aitken, Bram Bakker, Eric Bunge, Rex Burrow, Lennart Dahlgren, Mahmoud Eboo, Ralph Edebo, Ram Gidoomal, Keith Gilchrist, Mike Hamilton, Margaret Harrison, Ton Kunneman, Henk Mylanus, Torborg Nilsson, Alex Oechslin, John Painter, Mike Payne, Annika Sandstrom, Azad Shivdasani, Agne Svanberg, Max Weeden and Eckart Wintzen we would have no book to write. These were the people who invited us to work with their organization or team.

All examples quoted in this book have come from individuals with whom we have worked. Since we do not refer to them by name in the text, we would like to thank them here. They are Sunder Advani, John Ajene, Hans Barth, Andrew Blake, Tony Bradburn, Peter Bregman, Captain Chadda, Dara Contractor, Tony Cornel, Björn Dahlback, Peter Dawson, Maynard Donker, Leif Elsby, Foster Gault, Freddy Ghassens, Juhan Kohl, L. Lawal, Mike Laycock, Bengt Lindgren, Pramode Metre, Bill Mills, Henry Okolo, Alabi Olaleye, V. Ramchandran, Fred Ramundo, Danielle Roex, Graham Sanderson, Hans Scholten, Tony Smith, Willy

Söderberg, David Steavenson, Nico Timmerman, Alison Weller, Nicholas Wilshaw, Elisabeth Wistrand and Jose Zwiers-Smakman.

Then there are many friends and colleagues who have contributed to our work over the years. Here we would particularly like to thank Mark Brown for his exposition of mindsets, and also Chris Bakker, Hendrik van Beek, Tony Corke, Brian Durkin, Chris Elphick, Victor Marino, Ian Taylor, John Moss-Jones and Joe Sohm.

In preparing the early drafts of this book Anuradha Vittachi was of invaluable assistance in helping us get many of our ideas out of our heads and organized into a book. And during subsequent phases of the preparation, Lisbeth Almhöjd, Cynthia Alves, Mike Brown, Jane Henry, Mark Horowitz, Anna Pauli and Kate Vickers gave us valuable feedback and made many useful suggestions.

In terms of its production, this book represents a new venture, both for us and our publisher. Having written the manuscript on an Apple Macintosh (see the section on 'The Creative Story of the Book'), we decided we could not only deliver the book on floppy disk, thus saving all the time and expense of keying the text in a second time and then checking for errors in the proof stage; we could also, using our laser printer, produce camera-ready copy for the printers. This marriage of desk-top publishing with regular publishing allowed us to reduce production time by several months, and obviated any need for proofs. Joan Evans played an essential (and enjoyable) role in this, designing the page and laying out our text for the laser-printing. Her time, energy, commitment and suggestions have been immeasurable.

We would also like to thank Peter Gill for his input on the design, Tat Wasserman for working on the illustrations (most of which were also prepared on the Macintosh), Rupert Sheldrake for providing the illustration on page 90 and Malini Hettiaratchi for being continually willing to help whenever and however needed. A big thank you to Roger, Rita and Ken Nutting and to David Wynne for their kindness in allowing us to use their respective cottages on the wild coast of Sussex and in the depths of Suffolk and to hide away for three months with our Mac. Last, and not least, we would like to express our gratitude to our editor, Mary Butler, both for her patience and for her willingness to try something new.

FOREWORD

Man is a prisoner of his own way of thinking and of his own stereotypes of himself.

His machine for thinking, the brain, has been programmed for a vanished world.

This old world was characterized by the need to manage things – stone, wood, iron.

The new world is characterized by the need to manage complexity. Complexity is the very stuff of today's world.

The tool for handling complexity is ORGANIZATION.

But our concepts of organization belong to the much less complex old world, not to the much more complex today's world.

Still less are they adequate to deal with the next epoch of complexification, in a world of explosive change.

Stafford Beer (1975)

Fifty years ago management development was virtually non-existent. It was generally felt that anyone with the potential to become a good manager would naturally rise to the top. Then, after the experience gained in the Second World War with systems of management in the military, people started looking at what made a good manager in business. Could people be educated and trained in the art of management? And if so, how? This resulted in many of the military learnings being applied to the development of more professional business management.

The effect of this was a creative and dramatic step forward, changing the face of organizations worldwide. They have not only become relatively more efficient; they have also been able to grow in both size and complexity. The emergence of the multi-national corporation, for instance, has depended upon the efficient teaching, organization, and dissemination of management practices. This has allowed capital and labour to be brought into relationship in the most effective way possible, maximizing the earning capacity and profitability of the organization.

As this 'professionalization' has grown, so has the need for specific management skills. Most of these have been developed and taught by the many different business schools that have flourished. These range from the high-profile, highly academic university schools to the local college programmes that now exist throughout the world, in both developed and under-developed countries. Complementing these are a plethora of in-house management courses. The net result has been a revolution in the way organizations are structured, the way they conduct their business, and the way they treat their people.

In its early years, this emerging management science focused on the formulation and standardization of management practices. Its priorities were clearer and tighter accounting, better budgeting, long-term planning, more effective corporate structures, personnel organization, efficient production and the minimization of wasted time and materials. In the 1960s and 1970s marketing and market research became another important focus. And in the 1980s, information technology skills have also emerged as a priority.

Such skills were, and are, seen as the 'hard' skills necessary for the successful management of both corporate and public sector organizations. Yet, throughout this period, the more human aspects of management have also become increasingly important. Today, in larger corporations many managers spend much of their time managing other managers. These tasks require 'softer' management skills such as communication, leadership, delegation and motivation.

At the same time, increased decentralization, flatter organizational structures and demands for greater autonomy have meant that more and more responsibility is being placed in the hands of individuals. As a result there is also a widespread need for greater self-management. People need to manage their time better, learn how to cope with stress, balance their work life and personal life, and handle their relationships.

At the same time people are asking for greater recognition and autonomy. They are not willing to be managed in the post-war militaristic style and 'follow orders'. They are demanding to be treated as individuals with their own needs and concerns. Work is no longer just where they do a job, it is a place where people can express their values, their potentials and their creativity. For many people earning a good living is not enough; they also want an inner richness, they want to feel valued, productive and fulfilled human beings.

These are needs that managers must now take very seriously. They must find ways to bridge the growing need to manage the personal world of the human being and the intractable demands of highly professional management. This will require new attitudes to management and a willingness to explore unfamiliar areas.

Another factor with major implications for management is the increasing pace of life. As we move into the 1990s and beyond, we will, in all probability, encounter yet more rapid rates of change and uncertainty than today. Handling such a future will no longer be simply a question of more efficient systems and structures; these 'softer' management skills will become the new priority. The need for greater flexibility of thinking will become paramount. The organizations that will survive in the coming years will be those that are willing to let go of inappropriate attitudes and respond creatively to the pressures of change. This applies to all types and all levels of organization, from government and business to the family and the community.

These more human skills are far less tangible than accounting, marketing or computer skills. As a result they are sometimes seen as the poor relation of business management. Yet intangible as these skills may be, they are critical. They are the lubricant of any organization, and vital to its success.

When these more personal skills are taught, they are usually taught in a similar way to the 'harder' management skills. People learn 'how to' do them and go on trainings to practise their learnings. But the success of such approaches is limited. This partial effectiveness only serves to reinforce the view that such skills are 'soft' – there is little hard change to show for them.

The development of these skills requires not just training but also a much deeper understanding of ourselves. This means helping people acknowledge their own inner struggles, recognize why they sometimes react as they do, learn more about their own needs and motivations, discover how to manage their attitudes, appreciate their strengths and weaknesses, understand their own creative processes, and on this basis learn how to empathize with and understand the inner worlds of others.

Learning to tackle these more difficult facets of management is not an easy task. These inner dimensions are harder to see, harder to measure, harder to understand, much harder to handle, and even harder to develop. As a result little time has been spent exploring how to work in these areas. This is one reason why the 'training' of these self-management skills is so much more difficult than the skills with which we manage the world around us. In this respect, these are the 'hard' management skills of the 1990s.

As consultants, the message we receive from many corporate leaders is that the most difficult and compelling task they face today is to create environments that truly empower other people. In other words, to build organizations that respect individuals and allow them to release their innate creative potential. They also know that unless they do so they will not be able to cope with the complexity and changes of the future. They are realizing that difficult and hard to develop as these human skills may be, they are essential to our survival – individual, corporate, and perhaps global as well.

This is the new frontier of management science. Like all frontiers it is full of possibility. It is a place for explorers and people breaking free from outdated ways. It is uncharted and unfamiliar; yet it can be exhilarating and rewarding. It is a land of new hope. Like most new frontiers it is also fraught with hardships. Its pioneers are often met with scepticism and misunderstanding, and there may be many false starts and disappointments. It is also hard work.

In the next decade we expect to see more and more people dedicated to this new frontier, to the 'hard' skills of understanding both themselves and other people. The coming challenge of management science will be to re-vision the development of people, and raise the human audit to the level of the financial audit as a signal of the true health of an organization.

The task ahead may not be easy, but we are encouraged by the willingness of many people we meet to grapple with these 'new' hard management skills. This book is a small attempt on our part to respond to these people. It is a book for anyone who is concerned about how we place the human being at the centre of our future, and release the wealth of creativity that we all share.

The first chapter presents the context of the book. It looks at the creativity and other inner qualities required to manage ever-increasing change. Chapter 2 introduces the creative manager and his* role in the world today. We see that creative managers are not themselves new, but can be found throughout history. They are characterized by their willingness to look at their times through fresh eyes, and make their vision a reality. Today many people find a focus for their expression through organizations, for this is where they find the greatest leverage for their vision. The way of these creative managers is a way founded upon a deeper understanding of human creativity; in this respect it is an inner way.

The third chapter explores this inner way. It looks in depth at the various phases of the creative process that runs throughout our lives. We considered writing each phase as a separate chapter, but decided instead to present the process as a whole, emphasizing the dynamic relationship between the inner and outer aspects of creativity. Many of us currently have a good understanding about managing the outer aspects, but the more mysterious inner dimensions of the process are much more difficult to handle. These are the frontiers which we believe management science can now no longer afford to ignore. This

---

* The dreaded 'he' dilemma. As every alternative way of denoting the neutral pronoun that we have considered is either cumbersome or breaks the resder's flow, we have used 'he' througout in its androgynous sense of 'he or she' (except where the masculine sense is clearly intended), and sometimes 'she' in a similar neutral sense.

chapter is therefore the thread with which we weave the rest of the book.

In the fourth and fifth chapters we lay the ground for releasing creativity. We see how crucial it is to challenge all our assumptions and mindsets. This means being willing to look at the world through fresh eyes. It is about freeing ourselves to live in the present rather than on the basis of past attitudes and beliefs. Chapter 6 looks at the increasing pressures of living in a world of accelerating change, and at how stress can limit our creativity. It brings an important new dimension to the book. Stress is seen not only as a danger, but also as an opportunity – the opportunity to discover self-mastery. For the creative manager it opens another door on to his inner world.

Chapter 7 shows how the new frontiers of management we have been discussing, are reflected in the dramatic changes taking place in individual values. Increased self-awareness, so important for releasing creativity, is something that more and more people are exploring. It points to hidden opportunities behind the Information Age.

In some respects, Chapter 8 is the heart of the book. It is about a deeper understanding of our selves, and how that helps us manage the more mysterious aspects of the creative process. It is about listening to our own inner wisdom.

Creative managers are not just concerned with their inner realities: they are men and women of action. As such they are inevitably in interaction with other people. Learning to work with others is the foundation stone of any organization. The final chapter concerns itself with the hard work of applying our awareness and creativity in our relationships. We ask: How can we improve the quality of our communication? What makes a creative team work? How can others be empowered to become creative managers in their own right?

Although this book is written largely in the context of our work in corporations, and with managers in the conventional sense, it draws upon what is common to us all as human beings, and is written with us all in mind. It is based on our experience of life, and is written that we may each become the most creative manager in our lives.

Chapter 1   THE CREATIVE RESPONSE TO CHANGE

In a time when knowledge, constructive and destructive, is advancing by the most incredible leaps and bounds into a fantastic atomic age, genuinely creative adaptation seems to represent the only possibility that man can keep abreast of the kaleidoscope change in his world . . .

Unless individuals, groups and nations can imagine, construct and creatively revise new ways of relating to these complex changes, the lights will go out.

Unless man can make new and original adaptations to his environment as rapidly as his science can change the environment, our culture will perish . . . Annihilation will be the price we pay for a lack of creativity.

Carl Rogers (1954)

Everywhere we look we see change. Technologies change, scientific theories change, social customs change, values change, organizational structures change, people change. Indeed, it is often said of the current times that 'the only certainty is change'.

Change, however, is nothing new. It is intrinsic to life itself. What is new is not change, but the rate of change that we are experiencing. Never before in the history of humanity have our understandings, our technologies, our customs, our values, our organizations and people themselves changed so fast.

When we look back just twenty years, we see a different world – a world without personal computers, satellite television or cellular telephones; a world without the dramatic mobility and variety in jobs we have today; a world without Big Bang stock markets and global economic interdependence that affects even the smallest companies; a world with little awareness of widespread hunger, energy shortages and ecological devastation.

If we look back a hundred years, the world is hardly recognizable; no radio, no cars, no planes, no electricity, no electronics, no oil, no plastics, no cinema.

Go back a thousand years and we are in a different world altogether.

This trend towards ever-increasing rates of change is nothing new; it stretches back the length of human history. In neolithic times progress was measured over millennia; two thousand years ago it was measured in centuries; whilst today we measure it in decades. Indeed as much as change itself is natural to life, so is the acceleration of change.

Each new idea created in our mind and each new technology established has contributed to further discoveries and breakthroughs, pushing growth on faster. The Industrial Revolution, for example, led to the creation of mass production processes, and increasingly refined manufacturing technologies. When, a hundred years later, we chose to start manufacturing computers and silicon chips, we did not have to re-invent factories or the high technologies involved; they had already been established. Consequently the Information Revolution took hold in a fraction of the time it took the Industrial Revolution to establish itself.

Moreover, the very nature of information technology means that it will evolve much faster than industrial technology. Information is much more flexible than matter. It takes a comparatively long time before a steel girder design needs major modification, but software programs can and do need to change much more frequently – almost from week to week. Major software innovations, such as 'windows' and 'icons', have, once they have proved their efficiency, spread through the industry very rapidly indeed. To mass produce a new program needs only a good copying facility, not a new factory.

However giddy the speed of change may seem today, we can be sure of one thing. Barring catastrophe and disaster, ten years from now the pace of life is going to be much faster than today – and another decade later, considerably faster still.

In short, change is not only natural and here to stay; its pace is increasing and will in all probability continue to do so.

CHANGE AND THE ORGANIZATION

These rapid rates of change are inevitably having a profound effect on organizations. Long-established corporations which have been unable to recognize or respond to changing technologies and markets have fallen by the wayside. The American railroads, for example, thought the future was going to be 'business as normal', but saw their trade walk over to the roads and airways. British shipbuilding, textiles and aircraft were other industrial dinosaurs, so well established on their path that they were unable to adapt fast enough when change speeded up.

New industries have been spawned almost overnight. Computer manufacturers, software houses, management consultancies and companies exploiting the potential of biotechnology have appeared like spring flowers. Some have survived to become household names, but many, after enjoying a rapid bloom, have quietly faded into history. Others, unable to get

more than a toehold in their rapidly changing and highly competitive marketplaces, vanished before they were even noticed.

Whereas twenty years ago a company might have taken a year
or two to deliberate major shifts in product and direction, today
decisions often have to be taken in months – sometimes in weeks.
Within the computer industry in particular there is often a race
to get the latest breakthrough in technology or software on to the
market before competitors, or to catch up with their sudden
surprise announcements. John Sculley, president of California-
based Apple Computers, is in a better position than most to
appreciate this phenomenon. In his book *Odyssey* he writes:

> Time compression has nearly crippled our ability to
> cope with change. Technology has made the world a
> smaller, faster place that penalizes the slow-moving
> and stable institution. Companies that can quickly get
> ideas and information through their organizations for
> discussion and action will have distinct competitive
> advantages over others.

Larger corporations may have the advantage of greater
momentum and stability, and may not therefore be so easily
swamped by change; but they also have greater inertia. Getting
a large multinational to change direction is like trying to turn a
supertanker. When an iceberg suddenly looms out of the mist
ahead, the need for quick decisions is paramount if the tanker is
to be turned in time. A smaller, more manoeuvrable craft can
take a little longer to assess the situation – assuming that it is not
in the supertanker's way!

This increasing pressure for quick reactions takes its toll on
organizations and individuals alike. Without the time to think
things through, decisions may be made more on the basis of the

past than of a full appreciation of the future, and often from a state of corporate panic rather than being 'cool, calm and collected'.

Ironically the very factors which demand new ways of seeing and new responses tend to limit our flexibility. Being under pressure can lead to feelings of insecurity. To have at the same time to venture into new unfamiliar ground can only increase this insecurity. The resulting anxiety can lead us to play it safe and become rigid in our thinking.

The growing complexity of many of the problems we face often means that no one individual has all the information and perspectives needed to make the best decision. Yet we often see asking for help as a weakness rather than a strength. When we fail to cope on our own, we may interpret our failure as a personal inadequacy. In some this can lead to defensiveness, dogmatism and an authoritarian style, in others to feelings of helplessness, depression and withdrawal – hardly the best states of mind for dealing with the demands of such rapid change. It is little wonder, then, that so many of the decisions made turn out to be short-sighted, inappropriate, incomplete, or sometimes just plain wrong.

In his valedictory speech in 1986 as retiring chairman of the Confederation of British Industries, Sir Terence Beckett decried the damage done to business by 'short termism'.

> We have to recognize that decisions in industry taken today will produce repercussions lasting not just through the next season or the next year, but through-out the next twenty or thirty years. Snap decisions made in the heat of a single moment can affect a business for decades.

At the same time as organizations are feeling the pressure to make fast, expedient decisions, the growing interconnectedness and complexity of world affairs requires us to explore the long-term implications of these decisions. Since this in-depth thinking takes more time, a conflict frequently arises between the pressures for a quick decision and the need for a good decision.

The short-term pressures always seem more immediate – that is their essence. Long-term needs, on the other hand, can always wait a little while. When, for example, finances are squeezed, then research and development, training, social programmes and other long-term investments are seen as expenses that can be cut back with little noticeable effect. They are the ones that can wait. The problem is that they are always the ones that can wait.

This applies to many other organizations, not just to business corporations. In the 1980s, governments in the United Kingdom, the USA and some of the other more developed and richer countries reacted to short-term economic pressures by cutting back on education, scientific research, welfare, health care and social services. This approach may well be valid from the short- and medium-term financial and political perspective, but whether or not it makes sense in terms of the long-term health of the nation remains to be seen. This is not to imply that the long-term perspective is necessarily the correct one – if short-term needs are not taken into account there may well be no long-term future – only to highlight the very real difficulties that face organizations as they try to balance these seemingly conflicting needs.

AN UNCERTAIN FUTURE

Change can be exciting and stimulating. It can trigger new ideas, fire us with enthusiasm, provide new opportunities, confront us with new challenges, and awaken us from our slumbers. Change can be the spice of life.

Yet it also brings uncertainty, and in doing so seems to bring us, as individuals, many problems. Economic changes bring changes in employment – and the threat of redundancy. New technologies bring new processes – and more things to learn. Scientific discoveries bring new ways of thinking, challenging us to let go of cherished beliefs. Social changes may threaten our established identity. Personal changes may affect our values, leading us to question ourselves as to what is right, and what is really important.

And there are longer-term uncertainties. What will the world be like in twenty or forty years time? Will we still be here? Will we have survived the threat of nuclear annihilation? Will there have been a total collapse in the economy? Will all the pressures associated with such a rapidly changing world have led to totalitarian states in which individuals are coerced into conformity through a multitude of technologies? Or will it be more like the future of William Gibson's novels in which cybernetic and genetic technologies have run amok, spawning brain implants to flash the time 'in front of your eyes', with computers battling to defeat each other's 'viruses', and factory 'grown' meat. Or will some 'new age' vision come to pass, and wisdom and enlightenment prevail, allowing us to clean up the mess we have made, live in harmony with our selves and all life, and manage our future with intelligence and care?

The truth is, no one knows – although many have their beliefs.

The outcome may even be one that none of us have yet thought of. John Harvey-Jones, ex-chairman of the British chemical giant ICI, is one captain of industry who sees this very clearly. In his recent book on leadership, *Making It Happen*, he comments:

It has to be possible to dream and speak the unthinkable, for the only thing we do know is that we shall not know what tomorrow's world will be like. It will have changed more than even the most outrageous thinking is likely to encompass.

CHANGE AND THE INDIVIDUAL

Whatever may or may not happen, the very uncertainty of the future promotes anxiety. We begin wondering: What will happen to me? To my family? To my pension? To my way of life? To my health? What can I do about it? Will I be able to cope?

Nor is it just the future implications of change that bother us. The faster things change, the faster we have to adapt, and the greater the pressures upon us. Take electronic mail, for example. In many contemporary high-tech companies all employees are linked together through their computer terminals. Instead of sending a letter or memo and receiving a reply a few days later, a message can be typed in – or in some cases, spoken in – sent across the world, and a response received within hours, or minutes.

This clearly confers a great advantage in business efficiency; but there are hidden human costs. There is no time to breathe. There may be demands to make decisions before all the facts are available, or alternatives properly explored. The level of personal contact may be reduced. And there are mounting pressures to access, digest and respond to increasing amounts of information. Managers at seminars rush off at the first break to the nearest computer terminal so that they can check whether or not their office has left a message. It is not always that they are eagerly awaiting one – often they are relieved to find there is none – but the availability of such instant access means they no longer have any excuse for not receiving and responding to the message. The result is that people are increasingly expected to behave like the computers they use, rather than the human beings who use them.

In addition, computers, fax machines, portable stock-quote machines, voice mail, and phones that can be used in cars, on airplanes and walking down the street have all vastly increased the speed at which communication occurs and business gets transacted. Tony Schwartz, writing in *Vanity Fair*, describes this 'acceleration syndrome' as

> a state of constant overdrive. There's more infor-
> mation than ever to absorb, more demands to meet,
> more roles to play, the technology to accomplish every-
> thing faster, and never enough time to get it all done.
>
> The phenomenon is most visible, of course, among
> those in fast-paced professions – communications,
> politics, Wall Street, and Hollywood – and in big cities
> that are themselves intense, especially New York and
> Los Angeles. But living at an accelerated pace isn't
> limited to major metropolises and high-powered
> professionals. Clerical workers who use computers,
> for example, report with increasing frequency that
> they find themselves adapting their own rhythms to
> those of the computer. For that matter, just ask any
> working mother and father, no matter how placid
> their temperament or high their income, whether they
> find themselves running faster to try to accomplish
> more and yet struggling constantly to keep up.

The faster change comes, and the less able we are to cope with it, the more vulnerable we are to stress. We each have limits to how much pressure we can take, whether it be physical, mental or emotional pressure, without showing signs of strain.

The cost to industry of stress-related disorders is enormous. In the USA as many as 100 million working days per year are lost through backaches, headaches, nervous tension, exhaustion, etc., with estimated costs in billions of dollars. In European countries the estimated costs, proportional to the population, are very similar. If we include health problems, such as colds, exacerbated by stress, the cost is much higher still.

Health is not, however, the greatest cost of stress to organizations. The cost of mistakes and poor decisions that result from a stressed mind can be many times greater. Stress also affects our relationships with one another. We do not give each other so much time or attention; we too easily get annoyed or impatient with people who do not do things as we would like, and generally communicate less well. The result is misunderstanding and frustration.

As the pace of life continues to accelerate stress is clearly going to become more and more of a problem. Writers such as Alvin Toffler have repeatedly pointed out that if we are to survive the future we must develop our powers of adaptation. We must become more flexible and see change as less of a threat. We must learn to ride the wave of change rather than becoming swamped by it.

Change will not go away. Our challenge is not to restrain it, but to respond to it in new ways – to be able to cope with the totally unexpected when it suddenly arrives.

CHANGE AND SOCIETY

The rapid increase in the pace of life is also having a severe impact on the world around us. Industrial society's hunger for energy and resources and the unprecedented amounts of waste it produces are already having major consequences for the world in which we live. In the future the repercussions of society's avarice will almost certainly become more alarming, and will have widespread social and political implications. While most organizations study economic and market forecasts in great detail, few take into account the fact that social and political change can shatter the most sophisticated forecast. The demands of pressure groups and an increasingly concerned and vocal general public are the very areas in which organizations are most vulnerable. Responding to these unprecedented and unforecastable changes in our environment is going to become a major task for every organization and for the people who work within them.

These problems cannot be ignored. Our growing global interdependence and the near-instant speed of communication have brought us face to face with the crises confronting us. Moreover, the size and complexity of these problems can, all too easily, leave us feeling overwhelmed, frightened and powerless. We seem to be in the midst of a massive breakdown, hurtling at breakneck speed towards disaster – and with nothing we can do about it.

Yet, deep inside, many people know that the individual, and only the individual, can change things. Whether they have been political leaders with a vision, scientists with a new idea, artists expressing the spirit of the times, journalists who have fought a cause, managers who have pushed through new practices, or teachers who have passed on inspiration to all of these, individuals have always been the instigators of change.

Clearly we cannot change the world by ourselves. Nevertheless there are steps we can take within our own organizations, whether they be our workplaces, our communities or our families. Our responsibility is to develop creative ways of thinking and acting that make the best possible use of the many opportunities opened up by the constant change and innovation of our present-day world. No one has responsibility for the whole organization; yet the more people that take responsibility for themselves and their immediate sphere of influence, the more the organization itself can change.

It is not that we cannot make a positive contribution; we are often well aware of what we can contribute. We do not lack the power to contribute; what we lack is knowing how to exercise our power – and the courage to do it. We lack empowerment.

How can we gain empowerment? How can we bring more courage and vision into our lives? How can we make more of a contribution to the organizations and societies to which we belong? How can we manage our worlds with greater creativity? That is the focus of this book.

STABILITY IN CHANGE

A key ingredient in our response to change must be inner stability. Riding the wave of change is like sailing a boat through rough seas into the teeth of a gale. The wind pulls so strongly on the sails that we are in danger of keeling over. Yet if we do not sail close to the wind we will be awash with mountainous seas. We are all sailors in this sea, facing the forces of nature, trying to steer ourselves and the craft we have created through increasing turbulence.

Sailors in this situation need great skill and understanding. They also need to maintain an inner calm. Most of us would rather sail with the sailor who has a deeper understanding of his own capacities and limitations, and an inner resource of calm and peace, than with one who only knows techniques. We know that in the face of complexity, uncertainty and confusion inner stability is essential. Only then can we respond naturally without over-reacting, knowing when to relax and sit back, and when to be active and dynamic.

At this time in history humanity is sailing into a very fierce storm indeed. No one knows what the future will bring, but it is almost certain that we will experience changes on a scale never experienced before. When they come, they are almost certain to be sudden and unexpected. It hardly needs emphasizing that an organization whose members can maintain an inner calm and stability in the midst of the storm will be much better equipped to ride the waves that are to come.

This is one of the most pressing needs of our times: to develop the capacity to be more at peace with ourselves; to find a still centre of inner stability and calm from which we can think and act with greater clarity and creativity.

FLEXIBILITY AND CHANGE

The future we are sailing into is unclear. Our challenge is not to prophesy how the future will be, or try to keep change under control, but to respond creatively to the unforeseen when it appears. This requires an open mind.

We must be able to let go of old perceptions, old attitudes, old ways of seeing, and take on the new with the freshness, vitality and freedom it demands of us. This is not easy. We must be prepared to question all our assumptions concerning who we are, where we are heading, what we really need, and what is most important.

Clearly those organizations and individuals most likely to survive the coming changes will be the most flexible and adaptable. We need to rise above the rigid thinking and fixed views that tend to trap us. While they may have served us in the past, they may all too easily restrict our perception of the present and the future.

As Gareth Morgan writes in *Riding the Waves of Change*,

> We are facing a future where we will see changes all the time. How do we organize our corporations to face change? How do we get that through to people? It's not just a communication's exercise, it's a mindset, it's a different way of thinking.

Inner flexibility does not conflict with the need for greater stability; they each depend upon the other. If we cannot maintain an inner calm we may find ourselves clinging to set patterns of behaviour for a sense of security. On the other hand, when there is peace within we are much freer to respond to change – and to respond more appropriately. Thus flexibility does not mean being blown hither and thither by the winds of change; when we are flexible we are like a tree in the wind – anchored firmly by its roots, yet able to bend with the storm.

CREATIVITY AND MANAGEMENT

Stability and flexibility are not only two key ingredients in the management of change, they are also intrinsic to creativity. The creative person is not thrown by new situations and new challenges, but is able to step back and look at the new with fresh eyes. To manage the future successfully requires new thinking, and a preparedness to look at new responses. The unprecedented changes that humanity will undergo as we move through the 1990s and into the first decades of the twenty-first century will demand that we draw upon our creative resources as never before. This is the imperative that humanity faces as we stand on the threshold of the most uncertain future ever encountered.

We can be masters of our own destiny. But to use that mastery wisely we must draw deeply upon the creative spirit that lives within us all. We must become conscious co-creators of our future, steering ourselves carefully through the turbulent seas ahead. We must learn to manage our future with inner stability, flexibility and deep creativity.

This book is about drawing upon that well of creativity, and using it to empower ourselves and those around us. It is not just about understanding creativity; it is about allowing the creativity within to infuse our lives. It is about understanding ourselves, and understanding life. For creativity is intrinsic to life.

This book is also about us as managers – and not just those normally labelled as managers. Management, in its most general sense, may be defined as 'the optimization of resources'. In this respect we are all managers. We are all seeking to optimize the resources available to us. Whether we are managing staff in a company, managing a production line, managing financial resources, managing a farm, managing a home, managing our relationships, managing our lives or managing ourselves, there is hardly ever a moment when we are not managing in one way or another.

Management is part of being human. Man, unlike other creatures, has hands (*manus*) with opposable thumbs. We can handle the world in which we live, and through our hands our creativity can flow out into form. We can create tools, and create changes far beyond those created by any other creature.

Yet with this extraordinary power comes the responsibility to use it with wisdom and care. We need to allow our creativity to flow through ourselves, and from us into the world, so that we can channel it for the highest good.

Chapter 2

WHO IS THE
CREATIVE MANAGER

Life is making us abandon established stereotypes and outdated views. It is making us discard illusions. The very concept of the nature and criteria of progress is changing. It would be naïve to think that the problems plaguing mankind today can be solved with means and methods which were applied or seemed to work in the past . . .

Today we face a different world for which we must seek a different road to the future. In seeking it, we must, of course, draw upon the accumulated experience and yet be aware of the fundamental differences between the situation yesterday and what we are facing today.

Mikhail Gorbachev (1988)

Becoming a more creative manager is not just a matter of practising new techniques and methodologies – although these may certainly help – it is also about becoming more aware of our own inner processes. It is about adopting a new style of thinking and perceiving. It is about learning to see ourselves and our problems in a new way.

As suggested in the previous chapter, some of the most demanding and most critical problems confronting managers in the years to come – whether they be managers of a business, a nation or a small community – will be those that stem from the global repercussions of contemporary civilization. These problems in particular will not be solved by techniques and methodologies alone. Their roots run deep into our culture, and mustering the creativity needed to solve them will require of us new ways of thinking about our world and about ourselves.

The challenges ahead are very real, and cannot be ignored. There is much to fear, and much to take care of, if we are to steer a safe course through these turbulent times. But perhaps the greatest danger of all is not seeing what lies behind these many threats, and reacting only to the surface issues.

We might draw a parallel with an individual whose health is threatened. Perhaps the skin is erupting in blisters, the back may be aching, there may be indigestion, fever and sore eyes. Certainly these problems need to be taken care of, but a doctor whose only concern was to get rid of these symptoms would not be a very good doctor. We know that, as well as attending to the surface problems, we need also to ask what is behind these symptoms. Perhaps there is a viral infection, maybe there is a dietary imbalance, or possibly there is some deeper emotional problem.

Similarly, the world in which humanity now finds itself is a world whose health is threatened. If we do not look after the health of our planet and the health of our organizations, we will have no future to move into. However, if we only focus on managing the world around us, we are failing to see the deeper challenge facing us. We are failing to recognize that behind the environmental, economic and social crises that we face lies an inner crisis.

If we are to manage our future with the wisdom required, we need to ask ourselves some deeper questions. What is it in our thinking, our values and our attitudes that leads us to respond to change in such a way that gives rise to all these problems in the first place? What is it in our thinking that leads us to manufacture a thousand times the quantity of nuclear weapons required to eliminate ourselves completely? What is it in our values that allows the richer nations to keep food mountains while millions are starving? What is it in our attitudes that allows us to continue to decimate the rain forests, the lungs of the planet?

A Martian, visiting our world for the first time, might well be excused for concluding that humanity was insane. Yet, as individuals, we know that none of us intentionally sets out to damage ourselves and our environment. Our own thinking appears rational, our values acceptable and our perceptions understandable. And yet these outer crises continue to perpetuate themselves.

Often our natural reaction is to look for the cause outside ourselves and to blame others for this state of affairs. But are those we blame any different from ourselves? It is not that anyone is intrinsically wrong; we are each trying to make our own world work. And we each have limitations.

These limitations are seldom outer ones. What holds us up today are limitations in ourselves. The real challenge of the present is an inner one. We need to discover what it is in our selves that allows us to continue to behave in inappropriate ways.

There is already a growing response around the world to this inner need. These are the millions of ordinary people who know that there must be a better way, and are seeking to express it in their lives. They are beginning to think differently about the world and about their lives. They no longer accept that they have to live like a leaf tossed on the sea of change, fighting to keep afloat. These are the people symbolized by *The Creative Manager*.

The creative manager is someone who is learning to think in a new way. He sees that there is potential for learning in each moment. Rather than blaming the world and other people for creating difficulties, the creative manager asks: 'What am I learning from this?' This is not always easy; but he recognizes that being open to learning is fundamental to life.

He recognizes that the present time demands a different response. He understands that it requires of him increasing inner stability, a growing flexibility, and a willingness to live with uncertainty. He is aware that these attitudes are essential to a deeper understanding of the creative process.

These three skills of thinking, learning and creativity are what John Naisbitt and Patricia Aburdene, in *Reinventing the Corporation*, call the new 'TLC'. They do not mean what we usually think of as TLC – 'tender, loving, care' – but a 'shorthand for learning how to *Think*, learning how to *Learn*, and learning how to *Create*. These are the new basics, the three Rs of the new information society.'

Outwardly, creative managers may not appear to be different from any other person. They will come from very different backgrounds and training. You will find them in every sphere of activity, at work and at home. They are recognized not by what they *do*, but by *how* they approach what they do. The difference is an inner one; it is a difference of attitude.

THE CREATIVE MANAGER THROUGH TIME

The creative manager is not a new phenomenon. Throughout history there have been men and women who, in responding to the difficulties of their times, have been willing to step back and challenge old ways of seeing and thinking. They were people with a vision of a new and better world, who dedicated themselves to making that vision a reality.

The Industrial Revolution was fathered by creative managers. The scientists and engineers who pioneered the new technologies of the time – James Watt, Josiah Wedgwood, Matthew Boulton, Erasmus Darwin, Joseph Priestley, William Withering and others – saw the potential that they held in their grasp. They had a vision of a new world; a world in which the steam engine replaced human muscle, factories were freed from their dependence on water power, earthenware pipes transformed public sanitation, transport was revolutionized by turnpikes and canals, the mechanical telegraph dramatically enhanced communication, and people could be released from the hardship of working on the land eighteen hours a day.

Empowered by their vision of how, in just a few decades, the quality of life could be significantly enhanced, these men decided to pool their energy and help each other turn their vision into reality. They founded the now almost legendary Lunar Society of Birmingham. Meeting once a month and corresponding regularly, they sought solutions to the social, political, economic, scientific and technological problems of an industrializing community. The Industrial Revolution was no accident; it was consciously created and managed. These people knew how to tap the inherent creativity within themselves and empower one another.

At the same time other creative managers were busy forming a new nation. The Founding Fathers of the United States of America – James Madison, Governor Morris, Alexander Hamilton, Ben Franklin (also a visiting member of the Lunar Society), George Washington, James Wilson – likewise had a vision of a new world. They wished to free themselves from the outdated political thinking of Europe and have a government that served the people, rather than vice versa.

Studying every political system in history, and drawing on the current 'leading edge' ideas of people such as Thomas Paine and Thomas Jefferson, they together produced one of the most creative systemic management documents ever written – the American Constitution. In doing so they created a new political system that set the stage for two centuries of growth and freedom.

This 'new' America in many ways symbolized the birth of future thinking. The Founding Fathers believed that tomorrow could be better than yesterday. This was a significant break from past ways of thinking, for the European monarchies, linked by bloodlines to the past, viewed the world of yesterday as the golden age.

Back in Europe, a hundred years earlier, the 'scientific revolution' had been heralded by another group of visionaries. Doctors and philosophers such as Robert Boyle, Sir Robert Murray, John Wallis and John Wilkins, with interests in the emerging 'sciences' of physics, medicine, mathematics and astronomy, met regularly in London to share ideas and help each other in their researches. Foreseeing the implications of this 'new experimental philosophy', they formed what was called the Invisible College. Out of this was later born the Royal Society of London for Improving Knowledge – more often known as simply the Royal Society – which for three centuries remained one of the most prestigious scientific institutions in the Western world.

Although not all their names have become as well known as those above, creative managers have been at work in all cultures throughout history. The issues they were responding to and the problems they encountered may have been very different, but these individuals knew that they could make the world a better place in which to live. They recognized that their time demanded new ways of thinking and seeing, and used the windows of opportunity open to them to manifest their vision.

THE CREATIVE MANAGER TODAY

Today we face new challenges. Our ever-increasing rate of change is putting unprecedented pressures on people, organizations and the environment. Never before have we had to deal with problems of such complexity and on a global scale – problems which threaten the future of our species.

Once more we are being asked to step back and look at our situation with new eyes. And again, a new vision is emerging; a world healed of its insanity. In all cultures there are people who seek to contribute to creating a better world. They express the emerging values of our times rather than the values by which they have lived in the past.

Whereas in the days of the Lunar Society the challenge was to develop and disseminate the 'freedoms' inherent in the new engineering, and at the time of the Founding Fathers to build a new land of political and spiritual freedom, today the challenge is to manage the awesome power of our own new technologies.

How this potential is used – whether or not it is used for the benefit of humanity as a whole – is controlled largely by governments and business. Of these two, business probably has the greatest worldwide influence. The impact of corporations such as IBM, Sony, BASF, Ford, Coca Cola, Nestlé, Boeing, Levi Strauss, BBC, Heineken, Nikon, McDonald's, Shell, Mitsubishi, Unilever, Saatchi & Saatchi, Price Waterhouse, Siemens, Johnson & Johnson, Avis and Disney can be seen and felt in almost every corner of the globe. Although some may see this power and influence as a great danger, they also present us with unrealized opportunities. Marjorie Kelly, editor and publisher of *Business Ethics*, suggests that business may be the last best hope for planet Earth:

If business has the power to destroy the Earth, might it also have the power to heal it? If business has the ability to ruin human lives, might it also have the ability to save them?

The answer may be yes. From many sectors – inside and outside the corporation, among academics, activists and new thinkers – there are signs that a new life-affirming paradigm is emerging for business. Just as physics is shifting paradigms of the physical world from matter to energy, and as medicine is shifting paradigms of health care from treatment to prevention, so too is a shift underway in business ... The new paradigm has to do, in short, with making a better world – and using business as a tool.

No, the millennium has not arrived. But there are signs that the way we think about business – and the way business thinks about itself – are beginning to change.

POWER TO THE PEOPLE

We should not forget that organizations are, and always have been, composed of people. It is people who make the judgements and decisions which determine the direction and actions of an organization. What we have to look at are the beliefs, attitudes and values behind the judgements and decisions.

Most corporate organizations evolved in response to commercial interests, and the people who worked within them made decisions largely in the context of those interests. What products have the most market potential? What will bring the best return on investment? What is in the long-term interest of the business? Such criteria were primarily financial. They did not consider the wider environment beyond the organization's immediate field of operation and the interests of its shareholders.

Today, however, the values and criteria that determine corporate direction are beginning to change. People are recognizing that decisions can no longer be made in isolation from their wider implications. There are personal needs beyond money and security that people wish to see addressed if they are to be satisfied in their work. There are social issues which have to be considered; growing numbers of people are feeling that they do not wish to work in jobs which cause hardship or suffering to others. It is being recognized that if people do not take into account the long-term environmental consequences of their decisions there may be no marketplace, no corporation and no work in a decade or two.

At the same time the power in these organizations is becoming more widely distributed. Whereas in the past a few people could be relied on to make most of the decisions, the complexity of contemporary organizations means that more and more people are being involved in decision making. People's desire to be heard, to be recognized and to be involved has led to management styles becoming more open. In addition, the structures of organizations are changing; hierarchies are becoming flatter and more flexible, often giving way to matrix and network structures. The net effect is that more and more people are having a direct say in the direction and activities of the organizations in which they are involved.

Thus the new values which are being expressed at an individual level are finding increasing opportunity for expression within organizations. And the far-reaching impact that organizations have on the world amplifies the opportunity for these growing values to find expression on a global level.

Whereas the creative managers of the past were those fortunate enough to have the position and circumstances to be able to manifest their vision, today organizations are offering a similar potential leverage to many people working within them. They are becoming the vehicle through which people can express their values and vision.

RE-VISIONING THE ROLE OF THE ORGANIZATION

One area in which changing personal values are beginning to have a significant impact on corporate policies is ecology. Environmental disaster is clearly not in the long-term interest of any company, yet the threat of it is so far removed from the considerations of marketing policy, annual budgets and corporate strategy that it rarely, if ever, enters boardroom considerations. But although it may not be an issue that is put on the table, it is an issue that is frequently in people's minds – from boardroom to shopfloor. Few of us can notice the dangers we face without being concerned.

The chemical industry, in particular, is beset by this conflict between company policy and personal concerns. It is, by its very nature, not very friendly to the environment. It can have problems with the effluents it produces; there can be dangers associated with production; and many chemicals are difficult to transport. In addition, the products themselves may have to be handled carefully, some may be dangerous to living systems, or they may not degrade easily once their job is done.

What happens when people working for a chemical company feel, as many do, a responsibility towards the environment? The needs of the company to survive financially may require that people respond in ways that are not always in the best interests of the environment as a whole, while, at the same time, the people may have a need to see their inner values reflected in their work life. One might argue that people who find themselves in this situation should leave and find work in a more compatible industry. But for most this is not practical; personal and family needs do not allow them the flexibility of retraining, they would probably have to suffer an unacceptable reduction in salary, and in most cases relocation would present severe disruption to family life.

An international chemical group with whom we were working found themselves faced with this conflict. A number of the employees, including some of the directors, wished to see the company adopt a policy of 'environmentally friendly chemistry'. They wanted the company to produce only products for water-based systems – products that were safe for the environment, the user, the public and the employee – and for these products to be produced by equally safe means. They believed that their company should adopt the goal of becoming, within five years, one of the cleanest chemical companies in the world. Other members of the company, including the financial director, felt that these objectives were impractical, to say the least. They argued that to attempt such a shift, given the current state of the industry as a whole, would be financial, and hence corporate, suicide.

The situation came to a head at the annual strategy meeting. Feelings were running high in both camps, and their positions were becoming increasingly entrenched. Rather than try to resolve the polarization by argument and debate, we invited them to explore together their different perceptions of the issue, including the advantages and disadvantages of the two proposals. This allowed both sides to step back from their position without feeling they were giving in, and enabling them to hear each other's concerns.

After a day of intense exploration, common ground was reached. Everyone in the room, from the president to union leaders, agreed that on a personal level they were not completely happy working in an industry that had negative environmental side-effects. The conflict now had a larger context within which it could be explored, and which did not leave people polarized. The 'pragmatists' were able to acknowledge the values and needs of the individual. And the 'greens', feeling heard, were in turn able to hear the very real concerns of the pragmatists. The conflict between the needs of the individual and the needs of the company was now a conflict everyone could share.

It then took only a matter of hours to agree upon a workable strategy. As a consequence, within one year, plants made significant reductions in emissions – and beyond those likely to be required by law. New research into more acceptable products is underway. Internal safety standards have been significantly improved. And, perhaps most important as far as the long-term alignment of corporate and individual objectives is concerned, a company-wide environmental education programme has been established. Although participation is on a voluntary basis, and is held outside work hours over a three-month period, 60 per cent of the total workforce has participated in this programme.

FROM GROWTH TO SUSTAINABLE DEVELOPMENT
It is not just the 'dirtier' industries which are beginning to include global and environmental issues within their long-term strategies. One of the largest computer manufacturers recently took significant strides in this direction, looking at their responsibilities towards the rest of the world. They are recognizing that business 'operates only with a licence from society', and that, in addition to its duties to its stakeholders, it has real responsibilities to the community at large, including the protection of the environment at local, national and global levels. This new thinking comes not just from a corporate need, but also reflects

the thinking of people within the organization. As the chief executive said on the announcement of a major support initiative for the United Nations Environmental Programme:

As a parent I have reflected on the sort of world my teenage son might live in when he's my age . . . Will it be the better, richer world that many statesmen and industrialists promise, when they marvel about man's achievements in technology, space or medicine?

Or will it be an infinitely poorer world: poorer in terms of pollution, literacy, urban disorganization; a world of continuing poverty?

Will it be a world where peace can prevail, when the requirements of an exploding population exceed the scarce resources of water, food and housing caused by rising sea-levels?

Will it be a world where we are forced to shelter from a lethal sun, unprotected by the ozone layer? Will it be a world whose economic system is in total chaos caused by the climatic changes?

Questions like these were regarded as alarmism in the 60s and 70s. They have become the realism of the 80s. Surely they must become the inspiration of the 90s.

Looking to the future, a growing number of companies are also beginning to appreciate that the notion of 'growth' that has fuelled corporations for years is now dangerously out of date. It limits our considerations to the physical dimensions of the economic system, that is, an increase in economic output. But as the Club of Rome made clear twenty years ago, such growth has limits. Growth is always limited by the environment, by the amount of resources available, and by its ability to assimilate waste. As a result all natural growths eventually taper off.

Today we need to replace the notion of 'growth' with that of 'sustainable development' – development being defined as 'a pattern of social and structural economic transformations; a continuing *qualitative* improvement in a quantitatively non-growing economic system'. This is what we all do as individuals. Our physical growth tapers off (usually before 7 feet), but our development as a person does not stop there; most of us continue to improve qualitatively – we grow inwardly. Some corporations are beginning to recognize that the same transition must now occur with humanity as a whole. To managers brought up on the idol of growth this comes as unpalatable news. It is, however, the only way.

SOCIAL RESPONSIBILITY

In the past business and the local community have often been in conflict. Images still persist of the company being the exploiter of the local workforce, while business has felt that the community was impeding its own growth. Nowadays, however, businesses are being increasingly asked, and could eventually be required by law, to play a major role in the well-being and the development of the local community. This may mean supporting community initiatives with money, time and people.

Most large corporations allocate part of their funds to charitable causes, but others go a lot further. Some have revived the old idea of tithing, giving part of their profits for the benefit of the community. Traditionally this part was one-tenth – which is what the word 'tithe' meant in Saxon English – although it can be anything from a fraction of 1 per cent to as much as 20 per cent. An American confectionery company, for instance, donates more than 10 per cent of its profits to local hospitals, schools, and other community services, including help for the homeless and for AIDS victims.

Anita Roddick, founder of the very successful international chain, The Body Shop, sees support of the larger community as a crucial element in the success of her company.

> We have discovered that our customers believe what we say, and that is one hell of a responsibility. You wear that responsibility more than you wear any-thing. What you do with it is to say 'How can I effect change for the better?' We try by bringing attention to such things as cruelty against animals ... and how the environment is being abused.
>
> I don't say we have found the answer. Every time we think we've reached perfection, the goalposts change. It's the searching for a better way that gives our company a stronger morale, a better purpose.

Those who see corporations only as self-preserving financial entities, out to maximize profit at others' expense, on first hearing of initiatives such as these often find it 'amazing that a company such as ... should be doing something like this'. But there are two things we should remember.

First, it is not the abstract entity of 'the company' that has instigated these changes. They have begun with individuals within the company who have wanted to see their values expressed. These people have, in most cases, then had to work hard in order to convince others that their proposals are indeed in the long-term interests of the business. Only then does the organization get behind it. As the manager in charge of the sustainable development programme in a major multinational remarked, 'Yes, such programmes are certainly good for our public relations, *and* they are also in line with what the world needs, and with what I need as an individual.'

The second thing we should remember is that it is not 'amazing' that these changes should be taking place through organizations, it is a sign of the times.

PEOPLE MATTER MOST

As growing numbers of people begin to express their human, social and environmental concerns, many managers find themselves struggling to cope. In the words of Tom Peters, 'Business ain't an abstraction. It is blood and guts human beings trying to figure out what makes somebody happy. We don't teach the value of that in our business schools.'

The situation requires a much deeper understanding of the people with whom we work, be they subordinates, colleagues or bosses. Even twenty years ago people were still regarded as an ingredient in production, and a cost. Lip service may have been given to the notion that 'people matter most'; but it ended at the lips. Very few managers ever did much about it. There were always too many other important things to get on with; and, more significantly, always easier tasks to tackle than dealing with the human being. But in today's work environment it is becoming increasingly important to understand the human side of the equation – and to a depth never imagined in the past.

This shift in attitudes is brought out clearly by Francis Kinsman in his book *The New Agenda*. In 1983 he visited thirty chief executives of major British companies and management commentators, asking them one question: 'What do you imagine will be the most important social issues facing British management by 1990?' They were given the assurance that no comments would ever be attributed to them personally, allowing them to speak their minds without fear of judgement from colleagues, staff or the general public.

As far as management development and training was concerned, two issues came up time and again. One, as might be expected, was the need for skills in information technology. The other was skills with people. Moreover, people skills were seen to be more important in the long term than information skills. As one captain of industry put it:

> In the good old bad old days, people used to talk about maximization of profit; then they toned it down to optimization of profit . . . Now you just can't get away with talking of profit unless it is in the context of every dimension of the human factor . . . Organizations must have a wider amalgam of talent at the top – and increasingly that will mean people who understand people in all their aspects.

Or as another said:

> There has to be some kind of educational process bringing the art of living into day-to-day management. There has always been a complete difference between the way individuals relate to their colleagues in business, and the way that they relate to their friends and family. In the latter area, kindness, tolerance, etc. are not regarded as sentimental and wet, but as making the relationship work. Can one parallel this in business now? The difference between the two sets of attitudes is beginning to narrow and that may be the answer to tomorrow's problems.

At the same time, people lower down in organizations are no longer content to be treated as lumps of flesh with time to sell. They are demanding to be treated as human beings with similar human needs as their bosses. This is leading to new corporate structures, less authoritarian control, increased decentralization and more delegation of responsibilities. The divisional manager of a medium-sized corporation put it in these words:

> Our hierarchies were unquestioned in the past, but times are different now; people are more educated, beginning to say, my needs are important too. That has changed our company in a fundamental way. The organizational structure is more human, and the personnel department has become one of the most important support systems in the organization.

In our own work with corporate leaders in Europe, North America, Scandinavia, West Africa and India, we see many who are passionate in their desire to see growth in their people, as well as their profits. They know that the corporation will not be successful in handling the future unless the untapped human resources are released, personal conflicts are understood and resolved, and people are empowered to make a real contribution. These leaders clearly have the vision, but often are unsure how to make it a reality. They find their past experience and training has not adequately equipped them for these new challenges.

This is how the director of the management training institute of a Scandinavian bank encapsulated this difficulty:

> We know we have to equip our leaders for the future, but even though we know this and have started a development programme towards this end, there is a

whole new dimension of working with people that we do not yet understand. When we can, we will then be helping people learn about themselves as people as well as learning how to manage.

Thus one of the key tasks facing the leaders of the future is to create a culture which will empower people, to learn how to acknowledge and accept individual differences, and to facilitate the development of creative relationships within their organizations.

Empowerment is often seen as something one can do to another person. We shall see in a later chapter that this is not so. People are empowered by an environment that gives them the freedom to express themselves as fully as they can. The leadership of the future is about creating such an environment, enabling others to become creative managers in their own right.

The creative manager values people whose ways of thinking go contrary to his own. He knows that each person brings different knowledge, experience, skills, attitudes, perceptions and abilities to a task; and that the best solutions draw upon the interplay of our individual wisdoms.

We know we need other people, we know we need to learn how to relate better, and yet many of us find this one of the most difficult tasks in our lives. Most of us, particularly men, struggle with issues around intimacy. We have learned to relate to people mainly on an external level, and have often hidden away the inner dimensions of our lives. We need to listen better to others, and also learn to listen to ourselves – to hear what we are really trying to say, to communicate our hopes and anxieties. The more we share our inner world, and our deeper caring nature, the more we facilitate our working together and empowerment.

THE ILLUSION OF MANAGING CHANGE

Organizations worldwide are beginning to realize that a key ingredient in responding to change is the development of people and their creativity. Many managers who have been brought up to think of organizations as machines are realizing that this view is outdated, and that organizations need to be considered as living systems. Managing change in these living systems demands a radically different approach to managing a machine.

In attempting to respond to change we tend to focus on managing its outer forms. Thus, faced with new problems, we try new problem-solving techniques. As the complexities facing us increase, we expand our computer facilities. If we feel the pressures of time mounting, we take up time management programmes. In order to control and handle change, we go on courses that teach us to plan better, become more efficient, and develop better communication skills. It is not that these 'outer skills' will not be useful; on the contrary, they are essential. However, unless the context within which they are used changes they will only partially work.

We have responded as if change is only 'out there' and as though this is where all our attention should be focused. The reason we do so is that we understand much more about managing the outer world. We are rather like the wise-fool Nasrudin in the following Sufi tale.

A neighbour found Nasrudin down on his knees looking for something.
'What have you lost?'
'My key,' said Nasrudin
The other man got down on his knees and began searching with him. After a few minutes he asked,

'Where did you drop it?'
'In the house.'
'Then why, for heaven's sake, are you looking for it here?'
'There is more light here.'

This is far more than simply an amusing story. It contains a lot of human truth. The key to many contemporary issues lies within us, 'at home'. We have lost sight of this, but rather than look inside, which for many of us is dim and uncharted territory, we look for the answer where 'there is more light', in the more manageable world around.

Similarly, we seek to manage change by looking where it is easiest. Yet, if we are to find the answers to the problems now confronting us, we must also look to the area from which they have sprung – our thinking, attitudes and perceptions. So long as we are caught in the illusion that we can manage change by managing the world around, the symptoms of not coping will continue. People will still feel overwhelmed and disempowered, and resistance to change will continue.

When new developments seem to threaten our established way of life we can become remarkably good at resisting them. It is as if we had a built-in programme designed to maintain the status quo. It is not that change is resisted for its own sake; it is resisted when it appears to threaten some of our deeper inner needs, such as those for security or control. This is why we fear and resist change. Until we understand that people are responding to a very legitimate inner threat rather than being bloody-minded, we will remain unable to manage their resistance to change.

This is why merely talking of the need to change, and setting up change programmes, is not sufficient to create fundamental change. However well-intentioned the policies may be, they are likely to meet with considerable resistance, or even failure, if they do not take the critically important inner needs of the person into account.

The basic blocks to personal change are, therefore, on the inside rather than the outside. To implement effective change we first need to understand the human being in much more depth. We must learn to listen to what is really important for others, and to their deeper motivations. As this happens people will feel more free and willing to change. Thus our goal must be to help the individual free himself from fear. This inner freedom is the source of true flexibility and creativity.

THE WAY OF THE CREATIVE MANAGER

Throughout history the creative manager has seen that a new way is required. Today the new way is an inner way. Moreover, because it is a personal way, it is a way that is open to millions of people.

The mark of the creative manager is not a different way of doing, but a different way of being. He appreciates that in order to manage the world around he must also manage the world within. He must learn how to manage his inner processes.

This way is about understanding our own inner worlds better. It is about becoming clearer on our motivations, and how we can satisfy them. It is about recognizing when we are angry, and having constructive ways of expressing it. It is about learning to listen, both to others and to ourselves. It is about seeing when we are stuck in old ways of seeing, and learning how to think afresh. It is about understanding the creative process, and knowing how to release it in our lives. It is about a new attitude to life.

Because this way is new to our culture, it is easily misunderstood. Sometimes it is dismissed as withdrawing from the world, a refusal to face practical issues. In reality it is getting to the heart of the matter – an archer would never be criticized for pulling back his arrow on the bow.

Even when its value is apparent it may be rejected as being too difficult. Following this way is certainly not easy. This is not because the way itself is difficult, but because it is new. To tread this path means standing up for what is true, and challenging past perceptions and beliefs. This requires vigilance, perseverance and above all courage.

When we do embark upon this way, we may soon become discouraged and give up as we realize that we are hunting in the dark. Because this way is new, we do not yet have many of the inner skills we need. We must seek them out, rather than continuing to look for the key only where there is light.

This addition of inner ways to our outer ways can be considered as a marriage of masculine and feminine values. To action we bring allowing. To doing we add being. To the alert mind we bring a caring heart. To our knowing we add the mystery of the unknown. To the desire for order we bring an acceptance of uncertainty. To technology we add people. And to the flights of our ideas we bring the ground of the Earth.

Our cultural conditioning has inclined us to overlook these feminine values. Industrial society and its organizations have been dominated by males and male values. This is one reason why the women's movement has been so important for humanity. It has forced us to look at this issue, and in so doing has confronted us with the imbalance in our societies and in our personal lives. Perhaps its lasting gift to us will be to evoke the feminine values within each one of us.

Most importantly, the feminine in us is aware that fostering creativity is not just a matter of techniques and skills. It is not that such techniques are not useful; on the contrary, they are most valuable. But as many of us know, even when we use these creativity techniques there is still something missing. There remains an underlying mystery about the process. What takes place is still beyond our control, and beyond our awareness. It is as though it has a life of its own which is always beyond our grasp. Techniques may take us to the door of this mystery, but, to enter more fully into the creative process, a new level of self-understanding is required. We need to learn how to trust and engage this hidden inner dimension.

The rest of this book is about beginning to understand how we can enter this mysterious process, seeing how it affects every facet of our lives and learning how to use it. In essence it is about deepening our understanding of who we really are, and how we live. For the way of the creative process is the way of life.

Chapter 3

THE CREATIVE PROCESS

> *The concept of creativeness and the concept of the healthy,*
> *self-actualizing, fully human person seem to be coming*
> *closer and closer together, and may perhaps turn out to be*
> *the same thing.*
>
> *Abraham Maslow (1976)*

There is a tendency to think of creativity as the province of a chosen few, the individuals who have been flashes of brilliance, leaving an enduring mark on humanity. In the thoughts of Socrates, Plato, Aristotle and the Buddha, of Aquinas and Descartes, of Russell, Wittgenstein and Bateson; in the art of da Vinci, Michelangelo, Van Gogh, Renoir, Picasso and Hockney; in the poetry of Shakespeare, Milton and Keats; the music of Bach, Beethoven, Mozart, Tchaikovsky and Stockhausen; the theories of Pythagoras, Newton, Copernicus, Maxwell, Einstein and Hawking; the inventions of Archimedes, Gutenberg, Watt, Babbage, Edison, Daimler and Buckminster Fuller; and in a thousand other celebrated names we enshrine our 'gods of creativity'.

In focusing on such people as creative, however, we imply that those of us who have not left such marks on history are uncreative; or, if we are, then just occasionally and mildly creative. In truth, while we may not be like da Vinci or Einstein, we are all creative – all of the time. It is just that some of us have used our creativity in ways that have left a visible mark, others have not.

'To create' means 'to bring into existence'. In this respect each sentence we speak is a creative act, a choice to bring a thought into a form that can be communicated. It does not matter that a thousand people may have independently come up with the same, or similar, words at other times; our act of creation is just as real. As you read these words you are exercising creativity; you are bringing images and ideas into existence in your mind. You are expressing creativity in every decision you make; whether it be in resolving a conflict, organizing a presentation, or preparing a meal. Whatever we do, we are causing the world to change, we are bringing new forms into existence. Every thought and every action we ever make is an expression of creativity. To be alive is to create.

VALUING OUR CREATIVITY

Most of us do not normally regard all our thoughts and actions as creative. We feel that 'real' creativity must bring into existence ideas and forms that are unexpected, that are 'new' in the sense that no one else has created them, and that have lasting impact on the world. But would a person who thought up the theory of relativity, without any knowledge of Einstein's work, be any less creative than Einstein? Would Einstein himself have been less creative if no one had taken him seriously? Certainly some of our creative expressions are 'new' to the world, and a few may leave a lasting mark, but in terms of the inner processes of the mind, they are no more 'creative' than any other of our creations.

If we judge creativity only by its external attributes – its originality and impact – we do ourselves a disservice. We do not see that creativity is, in essence, an internal process that is going on within us all, all of the time.

Once we get caught in the belief that we are not very creative, we are liable to fall into a self-confirming attitude. We may fail to see and appreciate our own creativeness, and unconsciously block its natural flow – proving to ourselves that we are not very creative. We may have the ideas but, believing we are not very creative, we ignore our own thoughts – because they are ours. Ralph Waldo Emerson put this remarkably succinctly in his essay *Self Reliance*:

> To believe your own thought, to believe that what is true for you in your own private heart is true for all men – that is genius. Speak your latent conviction, and it shall be universal sense. We should learn to detect and watch that gleam of light which flashes across our own minds. Yet we dismiss without notice our own thoughts; they come back to us with a certain alienated majesty. Tomorrow a stranger will say with masterly good sense precisely what we have thought and felt all the time, and we shall be forced to take with shame our own opinion from another.

How often have we found another taking all the credit for an idea that we had long ago? The other person is called 'creative', while our own ideas remain ignored. More often than not, we undervalue our own thoughts, keep them to ourselves, and do not act on them.

However, as we shall see shortly, the creative process involves more than just having a new idea; it is also about turning that idea into form. Edison is revered as the inventor of the light bulb. But he did far more than just have a bright idea; it took him years of experimentation, and hundreds of failures, until he succeeded in producing a bulb that worked. Those who trust their ideas, see the value in them and follow them through are those who express their creativity – and thus those we regard as 'creative'. Unexpressed creativity is not the creativity we seek.

A BLINKERED ATTITUDE

In those areas where we do express our creativity, we may often find it flowing along well-worn channels. A person may be a good cook, but not see himself as creative in other arts. Another may have many creative ideas in computer programming, but become blocked when she comes to managing a team. Another may express his creativity in graphic design, but not in solving problems. In those areas where our creativity flows easily and freely, we accept our gifts, often hardly noticing them. Yet we notice those areas where we are blocked, and again dismiss ourselves as uncreative. We again make creativity something special, beyond us, out of reach.

Like many other human attributes, our creativity can, in its early stages, be fragile and vulnerable. As children most of us were brimming with creativity, inventing new games, composing new sentences, creating new worlds in our imagination, making castles from scraps of wood, and making friends. Then we went to school, probably anticipating that learning too could be part of this creative play. Yet all too often the play was gradually lost. As we 'grew up', learning became more serious. Our creative potential often fell dormant, was sometimes denied, and for most of us lay channelled in a few approved directions. It is then little wonder that many of us finished school feeling some inner lack and disappointment. Free-flowing creativity became like a lost dream, a dim remembrance from the past now replaced by a highly developed aptitude for rational thinking.

A logical mind and a critical faculty are certainly assets, especially when it comes to solving complex problems. However, the creative process also draws upon the non-rational, unseen, mysterious aspects of the mind. An over-reliance on rational modes of thought can be a further block to our natural creativity. At its worst, our addiction to rationality can lead to a cynicism that denies any creativity whatsoever in us.

Creativity is also an attitude of mind. It is encouraged by an openness of thinking; by a willingness to live for a while with conflicting ideas, and not have the solution come immediately; by an inquisitiveness that looks for information and an eagerness to learn; by an appreciation of the workings of the unconscious and a preparedness to play with the imagination; and by a readiness to stand back and question assumptions and beliefs.

We often think of creativity as having a bright idea, a flash of insight, an 'Aha'. But it involves far more than that. It usually takes a lot of thinking, conscious and unconscious, before the inspiration can emerge. Einstein pondered on some inexplicable experimental results for many years before coming upon the Special Theory of Relativity. Nor is coming up with a new idea the end of the process. The new idea must be expressed and given form, and this too can take a lot of time and work.

Those whom we revere as 'creative' are, more often than not, those who recognize that there is a process at work, and who are willing to work with this natural process – while often the rest of us unwittingly get in its way.

CREATIVITY AS A PROCESS

To see the creative process in action let us look at some 'brain-teasers' of the kind often set as a test of 'creative problem-solving'. As well as trying to solve the problem, be aware of the process that is taking place, the stages you are going though. (If you know the solutions to all of them, see if you can recall the process you went through when you first solved them.)

PROBLEM ONE
You have a cake to divide into eight equal pieces, but you are only allowed to make three cuts in the cake. How do you do it?

Try to solve the problem before reading on.

You probably noticed yourself picturing the cake, or even drawing it, getting a quick feel for the problem.

And some of you may have seen a solution straight away. If you could not see it you may have experimented with some cuts, perhaps imagining dividing the cake into four equal pieces with two cuts.

Then you probably became stuck. Perhaps you went back and tried some different cuts, or maybe you just looked at it wondering how one more cut could get you four more pieces.

The longer you remained stuck the more likely you were to become frustrated. Possibly you even gave up, and decided to read on, or even look ahead for the answer.

Then suddenly, out of the blue, you may have seen how to do it. You realized you had made an assumption, and letting go of that assumption allowed you to see another way of tackling the problem.

And finally just to make sure you had indeed found a solution, you probably counted up the number of pieces and checked quickly that they would all be the same size.

(For those who are still stuck, one of the assumptions may be that the cake is not three-dimensional. Seeing through this assumption may lead you to a solution. Another assumption you may have made is that the pieces of cake cannot be moved around. Seeing through this assumption can lead to another solution.)

PROBLEM TWO

Although the problem shown in Figure 3.1 has been around for years, it still illustrates the creative process well. You are asked to draw four straight lines through the nine dots, without lifting the pen or pencil off the paper, so that all nine dots are linked, i.e. every dot has at least one line passing through it.

Some of you may know the answer to this. If so try and find a solution using just three straight lines – again no lifting the pen off the paper.

Figure 3.1

Once more, notice the process that goes on inside your head. There is the initial assessment of the problem, and probably some trial solutions. When these fail to satisfy the requirements you may do some re-thinking, followed by some more experimentation. Then there is perhaps a feeling of frustration as you become stuck – and maybe the feeling, 'Well, this proves that I am not very creative.'

As before, your frustration is probably the result of being stuck within a set of assumptions, a way of seeing the problem. Most people on initially approaching the problem 'see' the nine dots as defining a square, and unconsciously assume that the sides of the square present a boundary beyond which the lines cannot go. But no one said so. Try it again, experimenting with lines that end outside the square.

For those who know the 'four-line' solution, but remain frustrated by a three-line solution, a different assumption is almost certainly holding you up. If you are a good logical thinker, with a little mathematical training, you can even 'prove' that it is impossible to link all nine dots using only three lines. Proving it cannot be done certainly eases the feeling of frustration; but only proves its impossibility within a certain way of seeing the problem. You are probably 'seeing' the dots as points. This assumption means that you are trying to solve it with lines that go through the centre of each dot – but no one said they had to.

Those who want to give up are encouraged to do so. Read on, and see if the answer suddenly comes to mind later.

The phases that people go through in trying to solve problems such as these are fundamental to the creative process. Whenever we want to solve a problem, discuss another way of doing something, compose a report, build a new team, develop a strategic plan, discuss personal development issues, plan a holiday or redecorate the house, we follow a similar pattern. Even as you read these pages, and learn new ways of thinking and acting, the process is operating.

The phases may not always occur as such discrete stages, or in the same order. Sometimes they may occur so quickly we hardly notice them, at other times the phases may occupy us for hours, days or even years. Nor are the boundaries between the different phases necessarily clear-cut. Of the various ways of charting the creative process, the model that we shall focus on here is one that considers it as five phases:

Figure 3.2

PREPARATION is concerned with analysing the task, gathering data, looking for patterns, trying out ideas, questioning assumptions.

FRUSTRATION occurs when we are unable to resolve the issue, feel bored, irritated or despondent, and doubt our own ability.

INCUBATION is a time when we give up trying, put the issue on hold, and hand it over to the unconscious mind.

INSIGHT is the inspiration, the 'Aha', the moment we normally associate with creativity.

WORKING OUT involves testing the insights and turning them into form.

It is important to see creativity as a process such as this. If we only see it as the moment of insight, we are likely to undervalue the other equally important, although less striking, aspects of the process.

On the other hand, if most of our education and training has led us to focus on gathering information and analysis, then we again see only part of the process. We will tend to jump to the final stage before giving the less conscious aspects time to mature. If we are to allow creativity to flow more freely in all aspects of life, we need first to become more aware of the characteristics of each phase and understand how to work with the process as a whole.

PREPARATION
Starting the Way

'Genius', said Edison, 'is 1 per cent inspiration and 99 per cent perspiration.' Great authors sometimes spend years researching their subject. Some artists are renowned for the many preliminary and detailed sketches they make before embarking upon the final painting. Scientists may spend years designing and building a crucial experiment.

Yet most of us, in our everyday creativity, frequently wish that this were not so. How often, when starting to write a report, design a new programme or plan a strategy, have we felt daunted by the task ahead? We know that it is going to entail a lot of hard work; and yet what we would really like is to be able to bypass the 'perspiration', and get our ideas out quickly and effortlessly.

We know in our hearts, however, that whenever we have produced a work that we have cherished, the quality has come from the time and energy we put into the task, not just from the novelty of the insight. We also know that we can derive much joy and fulfilment from this preparation phase.

This phase has many different activities connected with it. When faced with a problem or beginning a project, we try first to get a feel for the issue at hand, size up the situation, and decide on our objectives. There may be several questions that need to be addressed. What parameters apply? Who else needs to be involved? Are there time constraints, or financial considerations, that we need to be aware of?

An early task in this phase is gathering together all the information that we need, bringing to light everything we know about the issue. If it is a project we have had an interest in for some time, there will be a lot of information filed away in the back of our minds, some of it probably quite hazy. The more we think about the problem, the more we can pull this knowledge into the foreground. People often report that having massed together all the information they have on an issue, they are surprised at just how much they already knew.

Data can also be gathered from other sources: from reports, articles and books, from other people who have some experience in the field, or from those who are closely involved in the issue at hand. A major decision may involve lengthy research, with a team of people working on the task; time- and energy-consuming as this can be, it usually pays off.

We need not be afraid to seek advice at this stage. In one corporation with which we were working, the director of a design team had to present a detailed proposal for the energy plant of a new industrial installation in twelve weeks. There was no flexibility on the deadline, and looking at all the research he had to do, he 'proved' that there was no way he could complete the project on time. He saw himself landed with an impossible task. On being probed he admitted that there were indeed other people in other divisions of his company who had already gathered much of the information he needed. Asked why he did not approach them for assistance, he replied that they would resent his taking up their time on this issue, and not be so willing to give him help in the future 'when he really needed it'. What he had not allowed himself to see was that now, as much as ever, was a time when he really did need their help.

It is easy for us to judge this manager as being weak, non-assertive or incompetent, and to find ourselves retorting, 'I would not have caught myself like he did.' But beware, many times the things that hold us back in the creative process are the apparently 'silly' personal issues such as these.

It is also a common experience that as more and more information is gathered our understanding of the central issue deepens; we begin to uncover the core of the problem, and see more clearly the heart of the matter. This deepening understanding can often lead us to see the issue in another light. Sometimes we may need to redefine the problem several times, each redefinition bringing us closer to the essence of the issue. In doing so, we may find that the real problem is very different from the one we have set out to solve. The importance of being clear on what is the real issue hardly needs emphasizing – the last thing we want to do is come up with a creative solution, only to find out later that we have solved the wrong problem.

Another part of the preparation phase is to explore trial solutions. The problem may bear similarities to others in the past. Perhaps the experience gained from solving them can help us in our search for a solution? Or other possible approaches may spontaneously come to mind. At this stage any possibility is certainly worth exploring; however, we should not forget that they are only trial solutions. Very occasionally one may lead us directly to a solution for the whole problem, in which case we can move into the 'working out' phase. More generally, the period of exploring trial solutions is an important part of expanding our awareness of the problem.

One aspect of preparation that is commonly overlooked is the need to become aware of and challenge the basic assumptions that we bring to the task. We are unconsciously conditioned by our past thinking and experience. Our minds tend to get stuck in fixed tracks, and limit the way we approach the task and the sort of solutions that we look for. An open mind is crucial to the creative process – so much so that Chapter 5 will be devoted to questioning our assumptions.

TAKING TIME FOR PREPARATION

In some respects preparation is something that is always going on. We are continually taking in new ideas, new facts and new experiences, any of which could be data for a future problem. This is why it is frequently found that 'more creative' people are those whose minds are always taking in new information – whether through reading, listening to lectures, watching documentaries or in some other way. This information may not be directly relevant to the work, but by expanding their general knowledge they are preparing themselves in a general way for problems to come.

The more deliberate preparation that we do when we settle down to work on a problem is a time to work hard with the conscious mind; a time to be unafraid of cool, critical analysis, mental clarity and rigour. This is not usually a great problem for the person who has been taught that these mental qualities are important. Most managers have been trained to seek clear and concise definitions of a problem, and to set objectives. They know how to gather data and how to analyse it. They are also very good at drawing upon past experience.

Where many of us fall down in the preparation phase is in our impatience. In our eagerness to get it over with, we often do not give ourselves time to explore the issue to the depth it requires. Instead we tend to seize upon possible solutions, and go for premature closure. Although this phase may be only one of five phases in the creative process, experience has repeatedly shown that, in general, the more time that is given to it the better the quality of the final solution.

When deciding how long to spend on the preparation stage, we tend to be torn between two contradictory choices. On the one hand, we find it hard to accept that however long we spend on preparation we will never have all the information we need. It would be more comforting if we knew we had thought through every eventuality, explored every avenue, and foreseen those surprises which are so obvious in retrospect.

On the other hand there is the tendency to want to get the problem out of the way. Almost invariably, this urge 'to get things done' takes priority over the need for a thoroughly thought through analysis. In most organizational settings this results in far too little time being given to preparation.

This almost universal tendency to move on to the insight and working out phases as quickly as possible is very visible in our seminars on creative management and problem solving. Our approach is to encourage participants to spend a lot of time focusing on the preparation phase – often as much as three-quarters of the total time of our work together. At first people find this difficult to accept; they feel they are hanging about and wasting time rather than getting on with the real job of coming to a solution. But this 'wasted time' is crucial. Not only are they gaining much deeper insights into the nature of the problem at hand, but during this period more appropriate solutions can appear.

The attitude we try to instil is one of creative restraint. The creative manager holds off going for solutions as long as possible – and then holds off a little longer, even though this may lead to frustration.

FRUSTRATION
Hints of the Mystery

The solution to a problem can, as we have mentioned, sometimes come during the preparation phase. An obvious solution may indeed work, past experience may contain the answer, or suddenly, as if out of nowhere, a flash of inspiration dawns. Occasionally the problem may be not so much solved as dissolved, as we realize that there is not really any problem after all. At other times, however, after we have done a lot of data gathering, a lot of thinking and analysis, and have explored all possible solutions that have presented themselves, the problem is still there and still needs to be resolved. In short, we are stuck.

An artist may find himself becoming frustrated when he just cannot get a face to express the feelings he wants, despite having tried again and again. A scientist may feel frustrated that she cannot get the solution to a set of equations, although she knows a solution must exist, and she has all the skills she needs. Frustration may hit a person writing a paper or a report as he begins to realize that it is not coming out right, that it is not expressing what he really wants to say. It may overcome people in a meeting as time moves on and the group is still no nearer a decision.

Traditional descriptions of creativity have tended to omit frustration from the process. Not being able to come up with a solution seems to be the opposite of creative thinking. In addition, the feeling of being stuck can feel like a barrier to our creativity. From this point of view, the sooner that we get out of frustration, the better.

Another very strong reason that we avoid frustration is because it is, by its very nature, uncomfortable. We may feel tense, irritated, angry, discouraged, inadequate, lost, bored, or very often simply tired and lethargic. We may imagine that we 'should' have the answer by now. We may begin to doubt whether we will ever come to a satisfactory solution. Or we may feel that, even if a solution exists, we will never find it in time. We do not enjoy being frustrated, and want to get out of it as quickly as possible – although, as we shall see shortly, this attitude may not always be the most useful way of dealing with it.

Not only may we feel discouraged by not having come up with a solution, but frustration can also manifest itself as a sense of personal failure, a strong tendency to doubt our own abilities and a feeling of inadequacy: 'I'm not good enough'; 'I've deluded myself, I am not up to this task'; 'I should never have taken this project on, it's clearly too much for me'; 'Someone else would have found an answer by now'. This is the time when we are inclined to say, 'I told you so, I am simply not a creative person.'

Even when we remain confident in our abilities, we may still feel some temporary inadequacy. 'I'm too tired and run-down at the moment to be creative'; 'I can't do this because I slept so badly last night'; 'I've got a mental block about this subject'; 'I am not in a creative mood these days.'

FRUSTRATION MISPERCEIVED

Frustration is a much misunderstood phenomenon. It is seldom allowed for or encouraged in our education. Ability is seen as 'getting on with the task', 'getting things done', achievement and success. Being stuck is a sign of poor ability. Instead of learning to recognize and handle frustration, students often see it as a barrier to success, a personal handicap.

A similar attitude is found at work. A person struggling with a problem tends to be asked, 'Haven't you done it yet?' 'Why do you find it so difficult?' 'Perhaps we should put someone else on the task?' The underlying implication is that struggling with a task and becoming stuck is wrong; only striding smoothly and easily towards an answer is 'right' and 'good'.

The net result of this cultural conditioning is to see frustration as a personal judgement, a sign of failure. We imagine that being blocked is the opposite to being creative. Yet were Michelangelo and Beethoven never blocked? Did Sartre, Wittgenstein, Russell and Pope never find themselves stuck? Did Newton's ideas always flow smoothly and easily? Van Gogh describes how frustration was a major part of his life. Einstein lived with it for years. Iaccoca at Chrysler felt at times that he was being thwarted at every turn.

Because we experience frustration so negatively, we 'mere mortals' assume that it is not part of the creative process. To many of us it therefore comes as a revelation to realize that it is. It can be a signal that something is missing, that something else needs to be done. Perhaps there are aspects we have not explored; perhaps there are hidden assumptions that have led us off in the wrong direction; perhaps it is simply time to step back and sleep on the problem. From this perspective frustration is a very important part of the process, which should be explored rather than pushed out of the way.

TWO TYPES OF 'I CAN'T'

Frustration, when it occurs, need not be seen as a sign of failure or inadequacy. It is not so much a sign that 'I am wanting' as a sign that something in the creative process is wanting.

At this point it is important to distinguish between primary and secondary emotions. A primary emotion is a description of a person's existential reality. The feeling that 'I can't solve this problem' may in fact be valid. Perhaps we do not have the necessary skills or training; perhaps a crucial piece of information is missing; perhaps we need help from people with strengths that we do not have. An advertising executive, for instance, may need help and guidance before he can resolve a difficult personnel issue in his department. Similarly, a good production manager would not necessarily be expected to be able to handle a complex strategic issue. In such cases the 'I can't' is a realistic assessment of how things are, of what we can do, and what we cannot do. These are feelings to respect. They denote a level of personal maturity in being able to acknowledge our own limitations. They may be a signal to develop our skills, seek more information, or get a little help from our friends.

Secondary emotions, on the other hand, are the real villains. They are based upon our neurotic fears from the past, and usually reflect an anxiety about our own self-worth. An 'I can't' that arises from a secondary emotion may be nothing more than a put-down of ourselves, a habitual tendency not to trust our own abilities. Such reactions are seldom valid, and certainly not helpful in the creative process. These are the feelings to step beyond.

To be able to separate these two types of emotion is important; it allows us to step back and listen to what the frustration is really telling us. We need to appreciate that it is a signal that can help us decide which way to move in our own creative process.

MANAGING FRUSTRATION

For most people frustration is the most difficult stage of the creative process to handle. Even those who know all about it, and understand its value, can still find themselves caught in it.

It is all too easy to react by pushing on regardless hoping for a breakthrough, or to jump to a snap solution. Often it is only in retrospect that we can look back and see that we were in a classic period of frustration, and that what we should have done was stop pushing an hour ago – or even a week ago.

Unlike the preparation phase, which is a deliberate conscious process, frustration cannot be handled by using mental skills and techniques. This is why it is so often misunderstood and dismissed. A period of frustration is a time when we really need to have trust and confidence in the creative process – and in ourselves. But, in our desire to get past it, we stop ourselves from seeing the frustration for what it is, a signal to stop – stop pushing, stop 'doing', and instead, listen.

This requires a very different attitude from that which most of us have learned and are used to. We tend to look for things to 'do' that will relieve us of our difficulties; but there is no stock solution to frustration. Any 'doing' will, more than likely, only make matters worse.

Frustration can feel like a mental wall that we are hitting against. It often seems that there is no way through. However, once we recognize that the creative process as a whole is an interplay of inner and outer processes, frustration becomes less like a wall and more like a permeable membrane separating the inner from the outer. What we have to learn is to pass through this membrane.

RECOGNITION AND ACCEPTANCE
When we hit frustration, we need to recognize that it is part of the creative process. We are then better able to see it for what it is. It is then also easier to admit it to others. As long as we regard frustration as a sign of inadequacy, we may fear that exposing our feelings of discomfort and 'failure' may also be seen by

others as an inadequacy in us.

Acknowledging our feelings of frustration helps us put them in their proper perspective, as signals to be listened to rather than barriers to be resented. In doing this we shift from being a victim of our feelings to being able to choose how we deal with them. Recognizing them as a message from ourselves, we can step back from the rational analytic mode of thinking, stop trying to push through, and instead ask ourselves, 'What is missing?' 'What else do I need?' 'Given that I am stuck, how should I proceed?'

We should learn to accept these feelings of confusion and uncertainty as a natural part of life. For most of us this is not usually easy. We feel much more comfortable if we know where we are going, and how long it is going to take. To hold our horses and wait, not knowing how long this discomfort will last, requires courage – particularly when all around us seem to be clamouring for a solution.

If we can hold this 'creative tension', and stay with it, we may sometimes break through to another level of thinking, a new way of seeing the problem. Perhaps information that we have forgotten suddenly comes back. Sometimes a clue can come from unexpected questions or misgivings.

HONOURING THE AWKWARD QUESTION

Bill and I were working on a lengthy report. We were well into the second draft when a feeling of unease gradually came over me. I began to wonder whether we had actually got things in the right order. This was disconcerting, for we'd spent considerable time organizing the material in the first place. The last thing I wanted to do was create a problem where none existed, particularly at this stage. I also knew that a major restructuring was the last thing that Bill would want to do. But I continued to feel troubled, so I told him what I was feeling.

Fortunately his reaction was not exasperation. He took my question seriously and we began to look at what would happen if we changed the order. As we did we became increasingly aware that the key theme, the message which underpinned everything in the report, had not been given sufficient emphasis. The problem was not one of order, but content.

In this case, although the question itself may have been unwarranted, it did nevertheless have a basis. It was a sign that another message was trying to come through. Had they ignored or suppressed the question, the chances are they would not have noticed the weakness in their report – or perhaps not until it was complete and submitted.

Thus, whenever seemingly awkward questions arise, we should honour them and give them space for consideration. Frequently the question will be a disguised expression of a deeper discomfort, a deeper frustration, which has not so far been fully expressed and does need attention. Acknowledging the nagging question, however irrelevant or foolish it may seem, can allow us to step back and open ourselves to what lies behind it – and what we find may be far from irrelevant or foolish.

ALLOWING FRUSTRATION

The crucial point about the frustration phase is that we need to re-vision it: to stop seeing it as something to get rid of and instead to allow it. We need to value it as a difficult but essential step in the creative process.

'Allowing' frustration does not mean walking around end-lessly doing nothing; allowing means recognizing it as a totally natural process, and learning to 'read' it for what it means. The better we know ourselves as individuals, the better we will know how to read the messages that our frustration is sending us. For a person whose staying power is slight, and who tends to hit frustration very quickly, it can be a sign not to give up but to persevere. For someone whose tendency is to go on and on gathering data in order to defer making decisions, frustration may well be a sign to stop for the time being and go on to the next phase of the creative process – incubation.

INCUBATION
Allowing the Mystery

A new-laid egg will not hatch on its own; it needs a period of 'incubation' during which the chick can develop to the stage where it is ready to break out. So, too, ideas often need to be incubated before they can hatch. And, as with an egg, this process happens out of sight; it is a development which takes place beneath our conscious minds. It is a period when nothing seems to be happening, all that we do is keep the ideas warm.

Incubation is a time to rest ourselves from conscious thinking on the task at hand; a time to leave the problem alone. It is a time for something completely different.

Sometimes we may enter incubation deliberately, knowing that after 'sleeping on the problem' we may well see things differently, or come up with fresh ideas. More often, however, we find ourselves pushed into it. Having spent a lot of time in preparation – and probably some time in frustration – we may say to ourselves, 'I can't go any further, I give up.' When the frustration is particularly strong, we may feel, 'I've had enough, to hell with it.' At other times the pressure of other duties and tasks may dictate that we leave the problem for now, and come back to it later. Or, we may simply be interrupted by others who need our attention for a while. Incubation can occur in brief interludes, such as going to get a cup of coffee, or over longer periods, such as a holiday or a week of focusing on something else.

However we may come to it, the essence of incubation is that we stop thinking about the problem, and stop trying to find a solution. The conscious mind is no longer occupied with the task. This does not mean that we have given up completely, although it may sometimes feel like it. The problem may be out of the conscious mind, but it is not out of mind altogether. It is on the 'back burner'.

Like frustration, this is a part of the creative process that is not always given as much importance and value as it deserves. It is not something that we are taught to do at school or in management education. In addition, our efficiency-orientated culture inclines us to see this stepping back and doing something different as a waste of time. Yet much can happen while our conscious minds are off the problem.

Many 'creative' people know that the quality of their solutions is greatly improved by handing the issue over to the unconscious for a while. The novelist Graham Greene, for example, deliberately gives time to this phase. Having completed all his conscious research, and gathered all the facts, experiences and impressions he needs, he does not immediately sit down and start writing. Instead he waits. He lets his unconscious mind take over, and watches what it has to tell him in his dreams. Only when the dreams have gathered and settled does he begin to write.

A rather different approach is taken by Seymour Cray, founder of Cray Computers. For many years he has been dividing his time between building the fastest, most powerful computers in the world and digging a tunnel that starts beneath his house. 'When I get stumped, and I'm not making progress, I quit. I go and work in the tunnel. It takes me an hour or so to dig four inches.' For Cray this is more than a simple diversion. Says the chairman of the company, 'The real work happens when Seymour is in his tunnel.'

A CUP OF COFFEE

Incubation can also be unintentional. We have all experienced times when we have taken our attention off a problem for a brief moment, and an idea that has been stubbornly hiding from us suddenly pops up.

> A colleague and I had spent the best part of a morning at a computer terminal working on the development of a new program. But the calculations involved were so complex that there seemed no way we could fit it all into the memory available. Every solution we tried eventually ran out of space. But we didn't want to give up; we both felt that it must be possible.
>
> In the end we decided to take a break and go across the street for a cup of coffee. We had walked down one flight of stairs and halfway across the street when suddenly the answer came. We solved it then and there. Over coffee we checked out the details and found we did indeed have a workable solution.
>
> Now I know that we could have sat at the terminal for another two hours and still not come up with this solution. But switching off for just half a minute was enough to give a new approach time to surface. In some way I must have known the solution all along, but without this stepping back it could not get through.

Stopping for a cup of tea or coffee is just one way we can allow incubation. Others include playing with the kids, going for a meal, and taking the dog or ourselves for a walk. Some people talk to other people as a distraction, others read newspapers or watch old films on TV. A great many people switch right off and go to sleep. Others soothe themselves with a massage, take a bath, or meditate. But the most common, and perhaps least noticeable, form of incubation is simply getting on with something else that needs to be done.

LISTENING TO OUR UNCONSCIOUS

Incubation is essential to accessing our full creativity. In letting go of the problem, we allow deeper areas of the mind to go to work, and they can often show us things we could not see so long as we were busy thinking consciously about the problem, or were caught up in frustration.

These inner knowings cannot always be put into words – which is one reason why our rational, analytic thinking prevents us from seeing them. When they do come through, they often appear as a feeling or an emotion. We may begin to become aware of misgivings we have about the route we are taking. We may notice a niggling feeling that more information or more analysis is needed. Or we may discover an underlying sense of acceptance about an issue which puts an earlier frustration into perspective.

Allowing deeper feelings to surface in a period of incubation can be invaluable in resolving problems in our personal lives. During periods of total frustration, it may be the act of taking space and time that brings about a turning point. For example, a marriage may be going through a rocky period. Having tried everything they can think of to resolve the crisis, one of the partners may sense the need to get away somewhere quiet – in the countryside, by the sea, or in the mountains. In this unhurried environment, devoid of the usual pressures, it may be possible for new and clearer perceptions of the relationship to emerge, almost unbidden.

SLEEP AND DREAMS

Sleep is one of the best incubators, for then the activity of the conscious rational mind is at its lowest. Not only may we wake in the morning with new perspectives on a task, but the unconscious may also speak to us in our dreams. Sometimes we may find ourselves dreaming about the problem, and our dreams may show us aspects of the situation we had not seen before.

Philip Goldberg, in *The Intuitive Edge*, vividly describes how the inventor Elias Howe dreamt the key to completing a workable sewing machine.

> Howe had labored for several years and was one small detail away from his goal. Then one night he dreamed he had been captured by a tribe of savages whose leader had commanded him to finish his machine or else be executed. In the dream the terrified inventor was surrounded by warriors leading him to his death when he suddenly noticed that his antagonists' spears had eye-shaped holes near the points. Howe awakened from his dream and whittled a model of the needle with a hole near the point instead of in the middle of the shank.

Some people find it useful to keep a dream diary, particularly when there is a major problem hanging around. Going back over our dreams can reveal inner responses and feelings that we never allow ourselves to see while we are awake – and rational. This is not a question of deep analysis, but simply looking to see what we are trying to say to ourselves in our dreams. In this respect we can unravel our dreams better than anyone else can. We have created the dreams; they are our symbolism, our interpretation. We have the key to understanding them.

GIVING TIME FOR INCUBATION

Letting go to this phase is not always as easy as it might sound. We are so trained to think with our conscious minds, and so consumed by the idea of getting to our goal in the shortest possible time, that most of us find it very difficult to stop thinking about a problem. Moreover, the more we get stuck in frustration the harder it can be to stop worrying about finding a solution.

All too easily, when the pressure is on us, it seems that we cannot possibly afford to take time off. Every minute seems precious. Yet, if the task is not going as smoothly or as quickly as we would like, the chances are that there is something else we know inside that is not getting through. The truth is, these are probably the very times when we cannot afford not to step back for a few minutes.

Others' demands for an immediate decision can also make incubation difficult. We have all received telephone calls in which someone asks us to make a decision on some issue or other. Seldom do we take time to mull over the decision; instead we fall into the trap of believing that we have to give an answer there and then. But how often have we later wished we had let the question sit for a while before replying? The truth is, we rarely have to answer a question straightaway, just because someone asks us to. Most decisions will wait twenty-four hours. Those that cannot can usually wait ten minutes – time to take a quick stroll, or a cup of tea, and see what our inner feelings are saying. It is surprising how often new perspectives can come in just a few minutes on our own, without the pressure of someone breathing down our necks – or, worse, down the telephone.

Even when we know that a period of incubation may be just what we need, we still have to contend with others who may view our taking time off as a sign of laziness. This can be particularly difficult in a company whose culture is one of, 'We pay you to work, not dream.' Some organizations, however, are recognizing the value of giving people time to step back. A British television company, for instance, pays one of their gifted young documentary-makers to go away alone to a small country inn for a couple of days to clarify his ideas before starting his 'official' work on a film. The small cost of a bed and meals for two nights is repaid richly in the imaginative depth of the ideas that come to him during these solitary days of walking in quiet fields.

INNER PREPARATION

Giving time for incubation is as valuable and essential as giving time to the preparation stage. Indeed it could be considered as another aspect of preparation. Preparation, as it is usually defined, involves conscious, rational analysis. Even when this phase is complete, there may still be vital information to be gleaned from our feelings and our inner promptings – our intuitions.

In this respect incubation can be thought of as a period of inner preparation. If we miss this out, we miss out on a fundamental part of creativity. For creativity is something which springs from the unconscious far more than it does from the conscious. Our true potential is not just what we 'know' in the sense of what is conscious, it is also what we know inside. It is this inner knowing that we most need to tap. This is where both the mystery and the depths of our creativity reside.

A period of incubation can lead us in several different directions. We may realize that we need to gather more data, go back and analyse the situation in more depth, or return to some other aspect of the preparation stage. At other times we may find ourselves returning to frustration as the need to resolve the problem makes itself felt. Often we find new ideas jumping into

our mind, leading to possible solutions. When this happens we
have moved into a new phase of the process – insight.

INSIGHT
Solving in Mystery

The essence of creativity is the birth of something new. Ideas which were previously unrelated suddenly come together, and from their new relationship a new idea is born. A flash of insight appears. Suddenly there is a new way of seeing things; and new possibilities open up before us.

This is the phase of the process that we most readily associate with creativity, and the phase we are most attracted to. However, if we only see creativity as this moment of inspiration, then we remain helpless. There is nothing we can *do* to make an insight occur – it seems to drop 'out of the blue'. If all we do is wait for it to come, we are powerless victims of the process – and the chances are that nothing will happen.

The creative person recognizes that although the insight appears to come from nowhere, it actually occurs as a result of everything that has gone before. The preparation, the mulling over of the problem, the analysis of data, the soaking of the mind in the issue, the frustration and its signals to look deeper or explore inner feelings, and the unconscious processes which happen during incubation, all contribute towards creating a mental field in which the seed of insight can sprout.

Sometimes an insight may occur during the preparation stage; just thinking about the problem is enough to trigger a new idea. Very occasionally insights can occur in the midst of frustration, but usually the state of mind in this phase precludes such breakthroughs. Most often they occur after or in the midst of a period of incubation. When people are asked where or when they have their best ideas, most respond with situations such as in the bath or shower, in bed, at the point of falling asleep, or on waking in the morning, on the toilet, walking the dog, having a drink with a friend, after making love, playing golf or running. What is common to all these situations is that we are not 'at work'. We are usually doing something quite unconnected with the problem, and in a relaxed state of mind.

A new idea may be triggered by something totally disconnected. A senior information system's manager told how:

> It really came out of the blue! I was walking past the Natural History Museum when the word 'Savannah' came. The word soon became a very vivid image. The meaning of the image then clearly developed. It all happened in a few seconds.
>
> I remembered how, when I was twelve years old, my father and I visited one of the first nuclear-powered ships. On a deck below, the guide opened a hatch and through a plexiglass floor we looked down into the engine room. Down there was the mysterious, forceful, propulsive engine.
>
> Now, twenty-four years later, this memory of the ship *Savannah* spoke to me and triggered a new realization: I don't have to know all about myself to go forward. The captain of the *Savannah* doesn't know and understand all about the atomic reaction inside his ship. But still, he can navigate it on a foggy night in unknown waters.

In situations like these, the disconnected idea acts like a seed, combining with an aspect of the issue at hand to create a new synthesis. And it is this synthesis that gives birth to a new insight.

INSIGHT AND IMAGERY

In many cases insights come as images rather than words. When Einstein hit upon the key to the nature of light, he was not sitting at his desk solving differential equations. He was lying on a grassy hillside, looking up at the sun through half-closed eyelids, imagining himself to be a light beam travelling from the sun to his eye. That is when the inspiration occurred. And it occurred after years of mental preparation and a lot of incubation.

The chemist Auguste Kekulé, who discovered the molecular structure of benzene, had a similar experience. Until that time all known chemical structures were composed of linear chains of atoms, and like other chemists of the time he had tried in vain to fit the six carbon atoms and six hydrogen atoms of benzene into a chain that satisfied the rules of chemistry. One night, after a good meal and a couple of glasses of brandy, he settled down to relax by an open fire. Half asleep, he watched the flames twisting and curling upon themselves, and in his mind they seemed like snakes circling round to bite their own tails. He woke up with a start. Flames do not go round in circles, but carbon atoms in the benzene molecule could. It was a closed chain, a ring structure.

In a way Kekulé already 'knew' the answer. But his belief that it must be in the form of a chain was blocking him. Only when he took his mind completely off the task could his unconscious speak to him and show him what it knew – and it spoke in the language of the unconscious, in images.

In the cases of both Kekulé and Einstein we see examples of major breakthroughs. The more that an insight brings together everything that has gone before into a new synthesis, the greater the quality of the insight, and the more the situation is transformed.

Insights are not always solutions in the accepted sense of the word. A bright and enterprising sales manager had been given the task of launching a new product division in an area where the company was weak and needed to catch up with its competitors. A few months before the launch he had a bewildering experience. He had the image of his division as an eagle, which certainly seemed to fit his sense that it was strong, powerful, and a potential leader. But when asked to imagine going inside the eagle, he was puzzled to find it hollow and empty; there was nothing there.

Gradually his own inner knowing began to seep through into consciousness. He realized that his project was missing something fundamental – senior management commitment. They were giving it lip service but not the full financial and strategic commitment it warranted. As things stood, it was clear to him that there was no way it could work. He approached the board, and told them what he really needed if the launch was to succeed. But they could not hear him. After several attempts he decided to leave and join another company. His insight had not so much solved his problem as resolved it. Had he not trusted his image and explored what his unconscious was trying to tell him, he would probably have battled on, and failed far more dramatically. In fact, the new product division never did get off the ground.

Because insight is the stage of creativity that most people want to facilitate, many techniques such as 'brainstorming', 'lateral thinking' and 'synectics' have been developed. While these can certainly stimulate new ideas, they should not be seen as solutions to the problem of creativity. Their effectiveness is dependent upon the amount of groundwork and preparation that has gone before, and the willingness of participants to move beyond the surface level of thinking. Used as part of the creative process, they can be very valuable (as we shall see later); but used as 'solutions' to the 'problem' of developing creativity, they can be deceptive.

SELF-TRUST

Insight is the magic of creativity. It is totally mysterious, never visible, and always beyond our grasp. We cannot bring ourselves to insight, and yet it happens. It comes to us. We say, 'It occurred *to* me.' It is a moment of inspiration, when something 'breathes into' us. Our task is not to create an insight, but to be open to it and see it when it comes.

The key is a receptive state of mind. We may not be able to hunt insights down, nor may we be able to choose the moment of an inspiration; but we do have a choice over how we receive them when they come. We can either keep our eyes open, welcoming the new ideas as they 'drop in', or keep them firmly shut, preventing ourselves from seeing what our unconscious is offering us.

Thus self-trust is an important personal quality in this phase. So-called 'creative' people are not creative because they have more ideas, but because they trust their ideas, and are willing to explore them. Others tend to dismiss their insights: 'Oh, that's just my idea – it can't be worth much.'

Self-trust means trusting not just our conscious thinking processes but also our unconscious ones. Then we are able to listen to our frustration and hear what we are telling ourselves. We can let go to incubation, knowing that it is time to hand the problem over to our inner knowing, and value the images and insights which come into our conscious minds, seemingly from nowhere. Remember that Leonardo da Vinci's inspirations and Newton's insights came 'out of the blue', from nowhere, but they trusted them enough to follow them through.

WORKING OUT
The Way into Form

To have an insight is one thing; to turn it into form is quite another. Countless people may have marvelled at the colours in a sunset, but it takes the dedication and skill of a Turner or a Monet to capture that vision on canvas in a way that communicates with others.

Many of us may have had insights into the joy and beauty of life, but it may take many months of hard work before that insight can be conveyed in the words of Blake, Wordsworth, Emerson or Shakespeare. Other minds may have had glimpses into the nature of light, but it was Einstein who was prepared to follow his intimations through. Many may have had dreams of a personal computer that matched the needs of the 'user-on-the-street', but it was Jobs and Wozniak who got down to the task of making it a reality.

This phase of 'working out' – of working the insight out of the mind into the world where it may be perceived – is a key part of being creative. Without it the creative process is incomplete. It is not the number of bright ideas we have that makes a person 'creative', but how many of these ideas are worked out from the realm of ideas into the world of action. This is the mark of a truly creative manager: the willingness to explore his bright ideas.

Working out is a highly pragmatic phase of the creative process. It is here that the insight is fleshed out and clothed, and concrete steps for converting it into reality are developed and planned.

Until an idea is given a form, creativity remains unmanifest and unknown. Whether the project in question is as small a task as organizing a meeting, or as large as building a factory, or as complex as creating a new high-tech company, implementation remains as important a part of the creative process as any other. A creative manager must be able to communicate insights, and inspire others to want to put those insights into practice; otherwise they will remain no more than private bubbles, bits of untested theory, no better than fantasies.

Yet all too often this phase is undervalued. Many new ideas may be conceived each day, but very few are born into the world because we do not pay attention to how they can be implemented. Often we are so bowled over by the insight that we forget that we must turn it into form before it can have value. Having had a bright idea we tend to think that the creativity is finished; we overlook the fact that working out is as important a part of the creative process as preparation or incubation.

As with preparation, this phase takes time. We have to try the idea out, get feedback and make improvements based on this new data. In our culture, we are often admonished not to give up, but the admonishment is usually accompanied by a heavy moral overtone – as if persevering should be a burden, something that goes against our natural life processes. Not giving up can, however, be part of an exciting creative process, when every 'failed' attempt is a source of more information useful for perfecting the next attempt, rather than a cause for discouragement.

PHASES OF WORKING OUT

Working out can be considered in two stages. First there is the testing of the insight. Having trusted our own insight enough to want to follow it through we must now ask: Will it work? Does it satisfy the original requirements? Is it really an answer to the question at hand? How will it look in practice? This testing can take seconds; or it can take months of analysis, checking and exploring hidden implications.

It can often happen at this stage that what seemed to be a brilliant idea fails the test. We have to return perhaps to incubation, or more likely be thrust back into frustration. We may become aware of a need for more preparation: to go back and think more deeply about the task, gather more data or become clearer on our objectives.

This is what happened to Edison each time an idea failed. It was back to the drawing board: Why did it fail? What else is needed? What other approaches might work? It was only because Edison was not discouraged by continual failure, but was prepared to see each 'failure' as new data, and repeat the creative process time and time again, that he eventually perfected a bulb that worked.

Once again we see that the creative process is not a linear sequence of events, but a dynamic process, any phase of which can lead into any other, and which we may dive back into many times before a problem is solved.

Even when the insight does seem practical, the process is far from over. We need then to move into the second part of working out – implementation. This phase can be brief; filling in an answer in a crossword may take only a second or two. Or it can occupy us for a very long time. If we are setting up a new management structure, the implementation may carry through into many of our daily tasks as we deal with the unforeseen issues that arise in other areas, the personal concerns of those involved, and the subtle effects the changes may have on their relationships, communication and approach to work. If we are establishing a new marketing programme, the implementation phase may continue for many months or even years, as we ensure that our ideas are turned into practical results.

Implementation is a stage where skills, training, experience, aptitudes, tools and resources are of prime importance. A creative composer needs a good 'ear', a knowledge of musical theory, the ability to write music, experience of which instruments and voices will give form to her inspiration, and good instruments to hand before she can manifest her idea.

A creative photographer needs a good 'eye', the right film, a good camera, knowledge of how to use the capabilities of his equipment, experience of what types of lighting work best, and an understanding of optics in order for the picture to work out.

A creative manager needs skills in communication, an understanding of human motivation, an appreciation of individual strengths and weaknesses, a willingness to handle her own feelings, experience of which approaches are most likely to succeed, training in specific skills, and abilities in leadership and empowerment before she can successfully implement a change.

THE CREATIVE PROCESS IN MINIATURE

As we enter implementation we are entering the creative process again in miniature. Testing out the insight in practice gives us more information; if it does not work first time, we have useful information as to how to make it work better next time.

During preparation the problem was the focus; now, in implementation, the insight becomes the focus. The question now is how to translate the insight into reality. Here we may again come up against frustration, we may again retire into incubation for a while, and we may again have insights into how we can best implement our idea.

Moreover, within every one of these creative loops the creative process is operating. We may be stuck on exactly how to implement a certain aspect of organizational change, then suddenly come up with the idea of changing a particular person's responsibilities. Then we may dive back into the creative process again as we wonder how to communicate this in a way which is not perceived as threatening.

A flash of insight may come to us in the night, and we arrange to meet the person the next day to present the idea. Yet still the creative process is not far away. How to structure the meeting? What to say first? How to deal with the other person's concerns?

And even when we have answered these questions, our conversation will be a miniature, almost imperceptible, creative process in itself, as we take ideas and express them in words and gestures, occasionally pausing in preparation, experiencing momentary frustration perhaps, and, just when we are not quite expecting it, finding the right phrase popping into our minds.

In one way or another the creative process runs throughout our lives. Whatever we are doing we are never apart from it. It is something we are involved in day and night. Indeed, it is part of being alive.

CREATIVITY AS A PROCESS

Creativity is not something we are engaged in occasionally; it is intrinsic to thinking itself. Almost every thought we ever had 'came to us'. We seldom construct our thoughts deliberately; instead we prepare ourselves through previous thinking, have an intention of something we wish to express, and the idea 'pops' mysteriously into our conscious mind. To think is to engage in the creative process.

It is also, as we saw earlier, part of life. Everything we do is a creative act. We are constantly bringing new forms into existence. It is true that not all these forms are that remarkable, and may not normally be considered worthy of the term 'creative'; they are nevertheless founded upon the same essential process. The more that we come to understand the process at work, the more that we can work with it to produce the more remarkable acts of creation.

If we pay close attention we see the same process in the activities and moods of people, in their relationships, in their crises, in their breakthroughs, and in the way they live their lives. The more we trust this underlying process in all aspects of life, the more freely does the creative process flow. To be alive is to be creative.

THE DANCE OF INNER AND OUTER

We can also think of the creative process as a dance between conscious and unconscious realms of thought. Conscious, rational deliberation on its own will not come up with new ideas; nor will any amount of incubation, if the mind has not first been prepared.

A problem needs to be taken in by the conscious mind, and then handed over to unconscious mental processes. It is solved by a creative insight that comes from within. And the inner idea is in turn converted into outer action. It is in this final uniting of the inner idea with action that the marriage between inner and outer is consummated.

Yet, because the inner is, by its very nature, hidden from our awareness, we too easily overlook it; we come to rely predominantly upon the more tangible conscious realms of thought. Our materially developed and highly educated culture knows a lot about the brilliance and perception of the conscious mind. We have become very good at rational thinking, analysis and planning. We know how to work with ideas and manage our own conscious processes. But we have ignored the equally valuable unconscious processes. As they are mysterious and intangible, we have not known how to make use of them, and have left them on 'automatic', hoping that they will work for us and come up with the ideas. Sometimes they do, but more often than not, our dependence on the outer aspects of thinking leaves us stranded at the very time that we most need our inner help.

LEFT- AND RIGHT-BRAIN IN CREATIVITY

This dance between inner and outer is reflected in a dance between the two sides of the brain. Over the last few years much interest has focused on the extent to which the left and right sides of the human brain are specialized in different types of mental function. The left appears to be particularly good at logical rational thinking, working with numbers, linguistic processing, control of speech and writing, analysing the verbal input we hear and read, and thinking in words. The right side of the brain, on the other hand, appears to be better at synthesizing ideas and visual–spatial tasks, such as judging shape, seeing patterns and drawing pictures.

Although some more recent findings suggest that not all the differences are as clear-cut as some of the early researchers were led to believe – for example, some verbal processing may be carried out by the right-brain – this distinction has nevertheless caught the attention of many people, particularly with regard to the subject of creativity.

Observing that both imagery and the ability to synthesize thoughts are associated more with the right-brain, and that they are also thought processes connected closely with the generation of new ideas, it has been suggested that the right-brain is also the seat of creativity.

So far as insight is concerned, right-brain processes may indeed play a more important role, but to conclude that creativity itself is a right-brain process is making the mistake of seeing creativity only as a flash of insight rather than as a process of which insight is only a phase – albeit an essential one.

When we look at creativity as a process we see that both sides of the brain play very important roles. Preparation, focusing as it does on analysis, data gathering, logical thinking and under-standing, uses the functions associated with the left-brain. During incubation, when no conscious processing of the issue is taking place, it is difficult to say which side of the brain is dominating – most probably both sides are equally involved. Insight itself is, as already suggested, primarily associated with right-brain functions, while the phase of working out returns us to the logical, analytic, verbal modes of thought associated with the left-brain.

Thus we can see the creative process as an alternation between the left and right modes of thinking, which to some extent reflects the dive from the outer conscious mind to the inner unconscious, and back to the outer. It would, however, be a mistake to equate the right-brain with the unconscious mind as some have done. Both sides are open to our awareness; and there are undoubtedly vast realms of both which remain hidden.

In our society, however, we spend more time and effort focusing on the abilities connected with the left-brain than on those of the right. A traditional education dealt with the 'three Rs', reading writing and 'rithmetic, each associated more with the left side of the brain. Art, music, poetry, dance and other mental skills associated more with the right side were generally given a lower priority.

This bias is reflected in our everyday conception of a 'bright' person. When someone is said to have 'a good mind', we usually infer that they are good at rational thinking, understanding ideas and communicating articulately. On the other hand, someone who is very good at painting or playing a musical instrument may not be thought of as 'brainy', unless they are also good at left-brain thinking.

Although some modern approaches to education have broken this mould, many of today's managers were schooled at a time when this attitude was still prevalent, with the result that they are more fluent and confident in 'left-brain' skills than in those associated with the right.

This educational bias is another reason why many of us tend to focus on the thinking we know best – preparation and working out – leaving the insight to happen in its own 'mysterious' ways. To be more deeply creative we need to balance our left-brain skills with those of the right.

LEARNING FROM THE PROCESS AS A WHOLE

Learning to work with the creative process is not about learning new techniques; it is learning to trust the creativity that is already within us all.

It is a simple enough idea, but the consequences of this shift in perception are immense. It means that we can see ourselves as our own greatest resource. We do not have to wait for someone to 'put' something into us. Nor need we write ourselves off as not belonging to 'the creative few'.

We each negotiate the various phases of the creative process in a way that reflects our own individuality. It is important for us to become aware of the ways we respond to the process – and also to recognize and appreciate how differently others may respond.

At this stage it may be worth considering your own strengths and weaknesses in the creative process.

• In preparation do you:
spend enough time defining and redefining your problem?
go too quickly for a solution?
spend time questioning your assumptions?
or continue working at it when you should be taking a break?

• When stuck and frustration begins to rear its head do you:
step back and accept the discomfort?
listen to what is trying to come through?
talk to someone about your feelings?
push on, hoping you can break through?
take it out on others?

believe you are not up to the task?
give up?

• How easy is it for you to turn your mind away from a problem and think about something else for a while?

• Do you make time for incubation?

• In what situations do insights tend to come to you?

• Do you value your own insights, or too easily dismiss them?

• Are you full of ideas but seldom carry them through?

• In the working out phase do you:
really test your insights before putting them into practice?
plan and organize in detail?
monitor and get feedback?

• How easy is it for you to dive back into the process again, just when you thought you had got a problem licked?

• How open are you to the mystery behind the creative process?
Or do you tend to look for security in the past and in techniques?

The more we come to understand ourselves and our own relationship to the creative process, the more we begin to realize that the process is something we are working with and learning from throughout our lives. The more we learn from it, the more that creativity can flow into our lives.

Chapter 4

CREATING THE WORLD WE SEE

The real magic of discovery lies not in seeking new land-scapes but in having new eyes.

Marcel Proust (1899)

An essential aspect of creativity is learning to see things with new eyes. We all too easily look through the lens of the past rather than being open to seeing things as they are. If we are to respond creatively to the radically different times we are entering we must be willing to challenge our old ways of thinking, and learn to see things afresh.

We may think we live in the present, but how many of us are willing to see the world and whatever we are doing with new eyes? Valuable as our experience of the past may be, it has the nasty habit of colouring our view of the present and the future. How often do we respond to a person today because of something she said a year ago? How much is our appreciation of a film affected by what the critics say? How often do we assume the future is going to be like the past?

We should not underestimate how strong is this conditioning. Without our realizing it, the past haunts almost every aspect of our life. Nor should we underestimate how difficult it can be to step out of it. This is one of the key issues that corporations struggle with as they attempt to manage change. In the words of the quality control manager of a Scandinavian manufacturing company:

> How can we get the supervisors on the factory floor to change their ideas on quality? They simply don't seem to understand that we are no longer living in the past. I know they have the ability and the expertise to change the process and improve the quality if they wanted. The problem is in their minds.

This problem is not limited to the more developed countries. The group managing director of an African conglomerate told us:

> If we are to continue to be a major force in the 1990s, we will have to create a completely new management style and working culture in this group. I do not know if the power of the past will let us do so. It is people's attitudes that have to change; the rest will follow.

Even some of the leading-edge organizations appreciate how easy it is to get trapped in the past. A major Dutch software company, who have doubled their turnover every year for the past ten years, realized that, in order to cope with the needs of the growing market and the demands of the industry, they needed to break out of the old way of looking at corporate structure. They found that the optimum size of each of their working groups was fifty. Now whenever a group reaches this limit they spin off a new division. As one of their senior directors remarked, 'We have to continue to keep open to new ways of thinking and organizing ourselves, or we are dead.'

Similarly, we find many of the leading management commentators of today going to the heart of this debate. Gareth Morgan, in *Riding The Waves of Change*, asks,

> How do you encourage people to let your organization become flexible, to face the issues, so that you can approach a competitive situation competitively? How do you do it? I think it is critical . . .
>
> In the past managerial competence went hand in hand with the possession of specific skills and abilities, it now seems to involve much more. Increasingly, it rests in the development of attitudes, values, and 'mindsets' that allow managers to confront, understand, and deal with a wide range of forces within and outside their organizations.

HOW DO WE SEE THE WORLD?

Learning to step back and think freshly and flexibly is a key to being a creative manager. But it is more than just our thinking that is conditioned by the past; the whole of our perception is unconsciously determined by what has gone before. Appreciating the implications of this is new for our culture. Yet, if we are to manage our future with the creativity it demands, it is essential that we understand the mechanism of perception, so that we can release ourselves from the bonds of the past. To do so, let us step back for a few moments and look at how we see.

We know from biology how the eye works. We know that light comes in through the pupil, and is focused on to the retina, creating electrical pulses which are fed back to the brain. From this information we create an image of the world around us. But how does the mind create this image?

Consider Figure 4.1. What do you see?

Figure 4.1

What is happening in your mind as you try to make sense of the picture? First notice that you are once again entering the creative process. The visual data is in front of you, and you are probably testing different possibilities. You may also be experiencing a little frustration! Some may even have had an insight; you may see a snow scene, a map, a person, inkblots or some other object, while others still see just black and white shapes.

What is going on in your mind as you reach for different possibilities? Either consciously or unconsciously you are comparing the data in front of you with some previous experiences. You are hunting in your memory for a match. When something does seem to match, you combine the data with your past, creating an image which you 'see' on the page.

What we experience in our minds as we look at such a picture is in fact the normal process of perception greatly slowed down. Incoming data is neutral; meaning is added by our past experience, already filed in our minds. When new data comes in the brain tries to find a match with past experience. When it finds a good match, the mind 'sees'; it makes sense of the data.

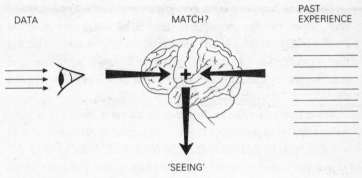

Figure 4.2

If you turn to Figure 4.6 on page 106 you will see another collection of black and white shapes. This time, however, it is easy to make a match with past experience, and the process of 'seeing' occurs so rapidly that you do not even notice it. It appears that you are simply seeing an image that is on the page. But you have in fact created the picture of a cowboy out of the data on the page.

Returning to the original picture, what do you now see? Probably you see the same image as in Figure 4.6. But the picture has not changed. You are seeing exactly the same data. What has changed is that you now have a past experience that matches easily with the data. The process of seeing is more automatic, faster – and obvious. It is the same creative process as before, but now much closer to normal speed.

Once we have made sense of the shapes it is hard to let go of the image we have created. It is difficult to go back and see them as a map, snow, inkblots or whatever else you saw previously.

But where has the picture you now see come from? It may look as if it is on the page, but it is, in fact, inside your head. You have created it.

The same happens with everything we 'see' – apples, trees, cars, paper, people, computers – as well as with everything we hear, smell, taste and touch. The brain is continually matching the incoming flow of electrical pulses with past experiences, and creating from this match an image in our minds of the world out there.

We create our world every moment of our life. This is creativity at its most pervasive level. And so powerful, constant and ubiquitous is it, that we do not even realize it is happening.

This may seem to be getting rather heady, and a little removed from everyday creativity and management; but let us hang on in there, the implications are far-reaching. They can relieve us from the domination of the past, and free our creativity.

MINDSETS

It is not just our sensory perception that is determined by the past. Once we have created a picture of the world, we then proceed to lay upon this 'reality' judgements, interpretations and evaluations. And these likewise are based upon the past. We see a certain model of car, then unconsciously judge its worth according to past reports and experiences. We may hear the words that someone says to us, then unintentionally interpret them in a way that is based on our feelings for that person. We may be interviewing someone for a job, and unknowingly evaluate them according to their accent and mannerisms.

These preconceptions we impose upon reality are known by psychologists as 'mindsets'. Mark Brown, a consultant who has studied mindsets and their effects on our lives in considerable depth, defines them as 'the psychological structures and schemas that make sense of our experience'. In everyday speech, mindsets travel under many different names – attitudes, beliefs, biases, values, assumptions, prejudices, judgements, preconceptions, stereotypes. Common examples of mindsets might include:

All politicians are corrupt.
People in business are only out to make money.
My mother still thinks of me as a child.
My children never listen to me.
Premarital sex is bad (or good).
Senior management is in control.
A good education will equip you for life.
Men with beards have something to hide.
It is difficult for women in business to get to the top.
My colleagues do not appreciate my real potential.
The early American settlers were hardy and adventurous.
People with Latin blood are warm-hearted and emotional.
The harder I work the more successful I will be.
English cooking is unimaginative.
Creativity cannot be taught.

People sometimes jump to the conclusion that to have mindsets is somehow wrong or unnecessary. In fact they are absolutely essential. Without them we would not be able to understand and relate to the world in which we live. We would not be able to process and evaluate new experiences – like trying to hang a hat on a wall without a hook. Mindsets are points of reference and anchorage.

A mind without mindsets is structureless, amorphous – as useless as runny jello. Imagine a manager trying to conduct an annual appraisal with a member of staff without any mindsets as to his performance, his strengths and weaknesses, and his potential for development. There would be no basis for making an intelligent evaluation.

Although mindsets are essential as current reference points, they are not absolute truth, only opinions. As such they need to be regularly updated. Running an annual appraisal on the basis of last year's mindsets is clearly foolish. Yet how often do we unconsciously allow this to happen, and thus remain trapped in the past?

We need to learn to step back and become aware of our own mindsets, and appreciate how much they condition our experience of reality. For the creative manager this is often the first step in developing a greater flexibility.

SEEING THINGS IN DIFFERENT WAYS

If we hold on too tightly to one mindset, we do not allow other perspectives to come into our minds – although there are many ways of seeing the same data. Take, for example, the illustration shown in Figure 4.3.

Past experience leads us to see these twelve lines as a cube. But we can do this in two ways. We can see it as a cube seen from above, or as one seen from below. Because we have been more used to seeing box-shaped objects from above than from below, most people find it easier to see it as a cube seen from above. But the other perspective is equally valid. With a bit of practice we can make it change from one to the other and back again without much effort.

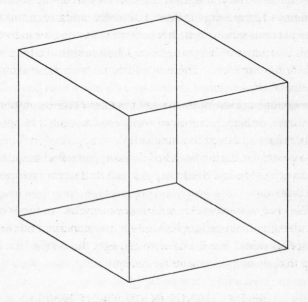

Figure 4.3

We might ask, 'Which is it really – a cube from above or below?' In fact it is neither. The data on the page is twelve lines. What is real is that we have created two different perceptions of this data. And moreover, we have created a three-dimensional solid out of two-dimensional information.

Similarly with mindsets, the same data can often be interpreted in two radically different ways. In a British TV advertising campaign, a national newspaper tried to put across the idea that, unlike other newspapers, it did consider alternative perspectives. The film showed a young 'skinhead' leaping on to a businessman – to attack him? Then the camera pulls back revealing a craneload of bricks that were about to fall on the businessman. The young man had pushed him out of the way just in time. The message is clear: it is foolish and dangerous to leap to habitual conclusions. It is important to step back and see if there are alternative views before reacting out of old mindsets.

We bring our own individual mindsets to every situation. Take sexual attractiveness, for instance. Western men generally prefer slender women; but is this just a matter of simple, physical 'chemistry', or is it the result of social conditioning? In other words, the result of a group mindset?

In a particular Pacific island community, men find large, fat women attractive and desirable, so much so that the headmen feed their women constantly, and prevent them from exercising, in order that the women become enormously fat. In the West such women would be hospitalized for gross obesity and their rolling flab would be viewed with disgust. But on the island, under the potent influence of the social mindset, these were the women the men found most sexually arousing.

Cultural mindsets also change with time. Plump Victorian gentlemen were considered desirably 'well-formed' in the 1870s. A hundred years later, trim athletic men were 'in', and being plump was out.

Another obvious arena where we find the same data perceived in different ways is politics – both national politics and the internal politics of a company. For example, when we see an argument between a trade union and a management team, which side looks and sounds 'right' to us is likely to depend on which side we were on already. Or, consider the newspapers whose views you choose to read. We like to think that we read unbiased news, but more often we read those interpretations which support our own bias.

At work we can have disagreements with our customers over the interpretations of shipping arrangements simply because their mindset focuses on delivery dates and ours looks at the cost of transportation. In a planning meeting the sales director may be looking through the short-term mindset of the next six months, while the marketing director is looking through the long-term mindset of the three-year strategy.

EXCITED MINDSETS

Some of our mindsets are so strong that they distort our perception of reality. We may have had the experience of buying a car which we thought was special and unusual. The next day we notice this particular car almost everywhere we look. It is as though the manufacturer had instigated a high-profile marketing campaign, tripling the sales overnight. When women become pregnant suddenly they see pregnant women everywhere. Or we come across a new word, look it up in the dictionary, and then see it everywhere as if it is the latest fashion. It is not that the number of cars, pregnant women or uses of a word have actually increased; but our mind is now set to see these things, and as a result we register incidents which before would have passed unnoticed.

Sometimes, however, a mindset can be so 'excited' that in our effort to match this mindset with incoming data, we actually 'see' things which are not there. Consider the brain-teaser beloved of children that plays on this tendency of the mind to jump to false conclusions.

Read the saying shown in Figure 4.4 on the next page.

Figure 4.4

What did it say? 'A bird in the hand'? Not quite – look again.

The mind, which is anticipating a familiar phrase, forces what is there into what it expects to see. Because young children read more slowly than most adults, and have less strong mindsets about such phrases, they are more likely to read the phrase correctly than an adult.

You may well be familiar with the following example of an excited mindset. Driving anxiously down a badly lit road at night, you may suddenly see a child about to step into your path. You brake, swerve a little – but then as you reach the 'child' you see it is only a branch of a tree, with an old rag hanging on it. Nevertheless, for a second or two the child was, for you, absolutely real. In times of anxiety and stress our minds are strongly set to notice those things we most fear, and thus unconsciously force and twist the data until it matches our excited mindset.

Advertisers deliberately play on our excited mindsets. By repeatedly placing an image of a specific brand before our eyes, they condition our perception so that when we go to the supermarket our excited mindset for that product causes that particular brand to jump out from the others. Once again, much of this process remains unconscious, and the processes by which we make our choices remain largely hidden from us.

GETTING STUCK WITH MINDSETS

Once we have a way of seeing things we easily get stuck in it. Our past perception can create an excited mindset for seeing a situation in a certain way. Often, however, the facts may change over time, but we fail to see what is new because we are seeing through an old mindset.

Consider, for example, the series of eight pictures, starting with the face below and continuing over the next three pages (Figure 4.5). What happens to your perception as you follow the images through to page 102?

Look through them now.

By the time you reached the last picture it will almost certainly

Figure 4.5

have changed into the figure of a woman. But when did you notice it was no longer a man's face? Most people spot the change around the sixth or seventh picture. If we were truly seeing each picture afresh, however, we should change from seeing a face to seeing a figure at the fifth picture. Having got the mindset that we are seeing a man's face, we hold on to this interpretation, and force the new facts into this mould even though it now better fits the image of a woman's figure.

Interestingly, when people have seen this sequence of images, and are then shown them in reverse, one by one, they now hold on to the mindset of the figure, and do not revert back to seeing the face until the third or second image at the start of the sequence – even though they know it will become the face of a man.

We find a similar pattern of mindsets becoming stuck and tripping us up in our everyday lives. Parents easily get caught in old mindsets about their growing children, often seeing the adolescent through the mindset they held when the child was 10. The same can happen with our partners. Like most people, they change with time, but how often do we hold on to our old views and not notice the changes they have made?

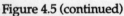

Figure 4.5 (continued)

This propensity to hold on to a particular viewpoint occurs even at our first meeting with a person, and can be pre-set by the smallest amount of information. A class of students at the Massachusetts Institute of Technology was about to be taught by a new lecturer. As an experiment half the group was told that the new lecturer was 'a graduate student in the Department of Economics and Social Science here at MIT. He has had three semesters of teaching experience in psychology at another college. This is his first semester teaching economics. He is 26 years old, and married. People who know him would consider him to be a rather warm person, industrious, critical, practical and determined.' The other half of the group was given exactly the same information except for just one word. They were told he is '. . . a rather cool person, industrious, critical, practical and determined.'

Both groups of students then came together and sat through two sessions with the new lecturer. Afterwards they were asked to assess his performance. Surprisingly, those who had been expecting a 'warm' person rated the lecturer as substantially more considerate, informative, sociable, popular, good-natured,

Figure 4.5 (continued)

humorous and humane than those who had been led to expect a 'cool' person – even though both groups had seen exactly the same presentations. Evidently, what they considered to be their own individual judgements had in fact been governed by the mindset suggested to them. They had made him fit their model.

The above example clearly shows four main principles of mindsets in operation:

> WE CREATE WHAT WE SEE. The subjective perception of the lecturer being considerate/inconsiderate, sociable/unsociable, humorous/non-humorous, etc. is something created within the mind of the student rather than existing incontrovertibly 'out there'.
>
> THE SAME DATA CAN GIVE MORE THAN ONE REALITY. All the students sat through exactly the same lectures, but saw two different lecturers.
>
> WE SEE WHAT WE EXPECT TO SEE. The priming had given the students 'excited' mindsets, and the lecturer they saw matched their expectations.

Figure 4.5 (concluded)

MINDSETS ARE SELF-REINFORCING. These three principles together produce a self-reinforcing system. The students who knew the lecturer was a 'warm' person tended to see a 'warm' person, thus reinforcing their original mindset, and keeping them stuck.

MANAGING OUR MINDSETS

We have seen how mindsets affect our perception of the world. But their sway does not end there. They have an impact on our thinking and most of our behaviour.

Willis Harman, president of the Institute of Noetic Sciences in California, is very concerned with the relevance of our growing understanding of the mind to the problems and decisions facing humanity today. He writes:

> Probably the single finding with the most conse-
> quences is the discovery of the startling extent to
> which our perceptions, motivations, values and
> behaviours are shaped by our unconscious beliefs
> that we acquire from our early experiences and our
> cultural environment ... Once we have settled on one
> perception of 'reality' all evidence to the contrary
> tends to become invisible. As they control us, they
> limit our creative powers and block us from fuller use
> of resources potentially available to us.

If our mindsets have such a powerful effect on our perception and thinking, we might well ask whether it would not be better to get rid of them? The answer is no. Without mindsets we would have no way of structuring our perception of the world, no means of creating a coherent reality, no way to discriminate right from wrong, no mechanism for bringing order to our lives, and no basis for deciding what to do. They are, in effect, the windows through which we see the world – without a window we would see nothing. They are absolutely essential to human consciousness.

When people first become aware of mindsets and their influence, they often mistakenly assume that they are bad. Mindsets in themselves are neither 'good' nor 'bad'. The real issue is whether we are in control of them or they in control of us. The key is not to try to get rid of our mindsets, but to become aware of them and take them into account – to recognize which window we are looking through.

Our minds are set from early childhood, from our parents, from school, from the media, from our friends, and from the culture in which we live. Because each of us has had different experiences, we are set in different ways – we each look on to the world through slightly different windows. When we meet someone whose mindset on a certain issue is different from our own, we all too easily think that his mindset is wrong – and ours is right. Thus, 'Capital punishment is wrong', 'Communists are wrong', 'Paternal management is wrong', or whatever else disagrees with our own cherished view 'is wrong'! This is not to imply that all views of the world are right. The point is that we unconsciously assume our view of reality is the only view, and are not open to what value there may or may not be in another's mindsets.

Mindsets both serve and limit us. They serve us in giving our perception a frame of reference; and they limit us in so far as that frame of reference has boundaries, and what we see through it reveals only part of the picture. Thus in managing our mindsets we first need to become aware of which mindsets are operating in a particular situation. Then we have to ask ourselves, 'How does this mindset serve me, and how does it limit me?'

We may, for example, hold the mindset that 'my children should have the best possible education'. This serves us in that we send them to the best school we can, support and encourage them in their learning, and make personal sacrifices on their behalf. This mindset, however, may limit us in that it prevents us from seeing that our particular view of how they should best be educated may not necessarily work for them.

Or we may have a belief that all managers in an organization should participate in a certain amount of in-company training every year. This may serve the organization and most individuals well, ensuring that a basic level of development is sustained. However, it may stop us from appreciating that for some managers this may not be a valuable use of time, either because their own commitment to development surpasses that which the organization offers and these individuals would be better supported by being given time to further their development in their own way, or because some managers are no longer open to learning, nor want to be trained.

Having explored how a mindset both helps and hinders us we are then in a position to consider the question, 'To what extent am I the master of this mindset, and to what extent am I its victim?' When we are the victim of a mindset, it controls our seeing, our thinking and our behaviour – without our even realizing it. To be the master of a mindset does not mean that we eliminate it, or that we control it, but that we see it for what it is, a window on the world. We acknowledge how it both serves and limits us. And we take responsibility for the effects it has on us. To be the master of a mindset is to have the *choice* as to how it influences our seeing, our thinking and our behaviour.

Figure 4.6

Chapter 5   FREEING OUR MINDS TO CREATE

To raise new questions, new possibilities, to regard old problems from a new angle, requires creative imagination and marks real advance in science.

Einstein (1938)

Often we do not realize the strength of some of our mindsets. Think for a moment of something about which you hold strong beliefs – abortion, nuclear defence, AIDS, drugs, religion, capitalism, for instance. How strongly are you attached to that particular belief? What would it take for you to change your mind and hold the opposite belief? Indeed, could it ever be possible for you to change? As you think about this you may get a feel for the power and the hold that our mindsets have over us. It is this block in our thinking which holds back our open-mindedness and flexibility, and kills our creativity.

We often attach so much importance to our strong mindsets that we cling on to them tightly, as if our life depended on them, and as if we would lose everything if we were to let them go. There are many examples of our unwillingness to put them aside. Some people may believe so strongly that they have to keep moving up the promotional ladder in order to be happy that they become neurotic workaholics and never attain the happiness they seek. Others may hold on to the mindset that personal independence is of fundamental importance and that their world would fall apart without it.

To have mindsets and to get stuck in them is the most human of traits. Most of us have probably had the experience of discovering that we have trapped ourselves with the expectation that others should do something in the same way that we do. On recognizing how ridiculous this is, our natural reaction is to feel bad and criticize ourselves. But this does not get us anywhere – except to make us even more a victim of our mindset. On the other hand, we can, if we choose, master the situation by stepping back, smiling at how easily we trap ourselves, and begin to practise flexibility.

The truth is we are going to get caught again and again and again. The sooner we learn to accept this fact, and take our mindsets more lightly, the freer we will be to look at problems with fresh eyes.

CHALLENGING ASSUMPTIONS

So often when approaching a problem we do so predominantly through the blinkered eyes of the past, missing possible new dimensions or other ways of solving it. We automatically bring various mindsets to our thinking. These may be assumptions as to what the problem is about, assumptions as to how we should go about solving it, assumptions as to the nature of the solution, or even as to what the solution is. Most of these mindsets are unconscious, and it is often very hard for us even to see that we are making assumptions, let alone to stand back far enough to ask whether or not they are valid. This is the Achilles' heel of the manager facing the need to perform creatively.

Ralph Kilmann, in *Beyond the Quick Fix*, emphasizes the critical role that hidden assumptions play in corporate culture and decision-making.

> Assumptions are all the beliefs that have been taken for granted to be true but that may turn out to be false under closer analysis. Underlying any decision or action is a large set of generally unstated and untested assumptions. If some of these assumptions turn out to be false, then the decisions and actions taken are likely to be wrong as well. Assumptions drive the validity of whatever conclusions are reached. We should not let our important decisions be driven by things that have not been discussed or considered. Assumptions need to be surfaced, monitored, and updated regularly.

Mark Brown discusses these limiting effects of mindsets and assumptions on our creativity in his book *The Dinosaur Strain:*

> So many companies are stuck with yesterday's patterns of thought. They see the world, their market and their customers through a grid that worked some ten years earlier. Today's unprecedented rate of change calls for minds that never become set. The intelligent unset mind is what business must have and yet rigid mind-sets are more often the norm in many organizations.

A good example of how rigid mindsets can cause us to prejudge the type of solution that we look for, and miss hidden dimensions of an issue, occurred in a Third World agricultural enterprise with whom we were working. As the leading tomato paste producer in the country, the company was very concerned about maintaining its market share in the face of strong competition. The senior management team assumed that poor marketing was the essence of the problem. Consequently, they analysed their current marketing strategy in depth, looked for areas of weakness, explored how to improve it, and brainstormed new ideas. By the end of this time the team was well on its way to implementing a new marketing strategy.

But the managing director felt hesitant. Something was not quite right. At first he could not identify his unease. Then suddenly out it came – an almost heretical statement: 'Our product is simply not as good quality as our leading competitor's, and people know it.'

It dawned on everyone present that he had put his finger on the real problem. They were then able to see the hidden assumption about marketing. While they had been correct in judging that their product was losing its image, the root cause was quality. They all realized that in the back of their minds they had known about the quality issue; but since the whole discussion had focused on marketing, it simply had not surfaced. As soon as it was on the table, the team set about dealing with the real problem.

TEASING OUT ASSUMPTIONS

Sometimes the assumptions we hold may be valid in themselves, yet still prevent us from seeing important dimensions of the issue. For this reason becoming aware of our correct assumptions is as important as becoming aware of those which are false.

When working with management teams on projects we encourage them, as part of the preparation stage, to map out all the elements of the task, including everything that needs to be considered. Having done this, they then look at how the data is connected, and explore some of the underlying patterns and implications. At this stage people are usually so caught up with the task that they do not see some of the basic assumptions on which the project is founded.

The director of an international shipping corporation wished to expand his business by establishing an emergency air ambulance service. The reasons were partly to serve the large number of their own employees stationed abroad, and partly to diversify the business by providing a service to other international groups operating in the same countries. He commissioned a research study on the project which confirmed this was a financially viable business opportunity. Having made the decision to go ahead, he and his colleagues began to plan the implementation of the service, looking at aircraft needed, technical support required, personnel, marketing strategy to other companies and capital investment plans.

Working with him, we began to look for some of the implicit assumptions behind this project. To tease them out we asked a series of 'Why?' questions around each of the main areas of the project, and in particular around the central theme. 'Why is it important to have landing rights in central Brazil?' 'Because one of our main potential customers has its biggest mine there.' 'Why is it important to service this customer?' 'Because he will open the door to business throughout the world.' 'Why do you want to do this business in areas of high instability?' 'Because that's where employees are most vulnerable, and most in need of a service such as ours. And that's where we can really maximize our return on investment.' Here is a critical assumption around which the whole project had developed – the assumption that an air ambulance service would be profitable in these areas.

It is not that this assumption is necessarily incorrect. However, holding this assumption as an unquestioned fact prevented the director from seeing other dimensions to the project which needed to be considered. Once he had recognized that financial viability in these countries was an unquestioned assumption, some of the dangers associated with the venture became apparent. He saw the high risk of flying in these areas, the difficulty in getting charges repaid from some of the countries, some unexpected costs of running a mini-airline, possible maintenance problems, and the possibility of competition from unexpected quarters. Interestingly, none of these issues had been taken into account in the research study, which had only considered the market opportunity. The assumption that it could be viable had hidden these other considerations – and, paradoxically, posed a threat to the profitability of the project. By considering these other perspectives, the director was able to create a much more balanced and feasible venture.

This process of repeatedly asking 'Why?' is a key to teasing out hidden assumptions. It encourages us to look more fully into an issue and discover the deeper beliefs we are holding on to.

As in the above examples, these assumptions may be too narrow, shrinking the area in which we search for a solution. Even though they may serve us in focusing our thinking and giving us a goal, they can also limit us in that they may mask other significant issues which could contribute to a fuller solution. Breaking open these assumptions expands the problem in our minds, and creates a field that is ready to receive new and unexpected ideas.

BRAINSTORMING

Another approach to stepping beyond the assumptions we may

bring to a problem is the use of what is commonly known as brainstorming. The intention behind brainstorming is that people should spark each other off with large numbers of spontaneous and wild ideas, and in so doing come up with novel solutions that none of them would have thought of individually. A fundamental principle of brainstorming is to be non-judgemental – particularly of ideas that the rational mind says cannot work. It is these crazy ideas that can often trigger less crazy ideas, and these in turn may trigger workable solutions which would never have been arrived at had the group only stuck to sensible ideas.

In order to loosen up the group's thinking it is often useful to include people who do not know very much about the problem, and who are not therefore so 'set' on the type of solutions that will or will not work. Participants are encouraged not to be serious, and not to judge whether or not an idea has any value. All offers are noted down, and people are encouraged to build upon each other's ideas.

There are several variations on the basic brainstorming theme, and each can be useful in coming up with new solutions to a problem. Most, however, have an inherent limitation in that they do not get people to step out of all their mindsets about the problem they are working on, or the sort of solutions they are working towards. As a result they may miss many new ideas. Some people also find it hard to suspend judgement on the crazy solutions. The need for a solution is still in their awareness, and the 'serious' problem-oriented part of the mind often says, 'Yes, but ... this is just a crazy solution – it won't lead anywhere?' Thus they hold themselves back from gaining the fullest value they might from the brainstorming session.

MINDSET-FREE

In our own work with management teams we have gone a stage further than traditional brainstorming techniques, adapting processes developed by Mark Brown, Synectics and others. In our process participants do not even try to solve the problem facing them. Instead they work on a completely fictitious, and crazy, problem – but one that does bear similarities to the issue at hand.

DEFINING THE ESSENCE OF THE PROBLEM

The first stage is to formulate the problem clearly, and in an open-ended manner that does not preclude a particular type of solution. One manager had initially thought the problem facing him was creating new management positions for some of his bright young engineers. But when asked, 'Why?', he replied, 'So that I can co-ordinate the activities of a multi-disciplined design team.' How to achieve such co-ordination is clearly a much more open-ended formulation, and one which could lead to a broader spectrum of new ideas. Another person, trying to solve the problem of 'poor communication', redefined it and made it more specific by asking, 'How can I facilitate greater communication and feedback through a large hierarchical corporate structure?'

DEFINING THE ZANY PROBLEM

Having got a succinct and open-ended definition, the second stage is to think up a new fictitious problem which has no direct bearing on the problem at hand, but which does have a similar underlying nature. Thus the problem of how to co-ordinate the activities of the multi-disciplined design team might be 'translated' as, 'How does one get a pile of rocks to sing in tune?' And the problem of how to facilitate greater communication and feedback through a large hierarchical corporate structure might be turned into the question, 'How does an octopus gather in grains of gold dust?' These may seem ridiculous and unreal questions, zany and far-removed from the real problem; but that is their value. As they are so far-removed, the mind is far less likely to be judging (either consciously or unconsciously) whether or not a particular idea is really workable or not. The important thing is that the fictitious problem bears some general parallels to the real problem.

ANALYSING THE FICTITIOUS PROBLEM

Having obtained a good 'new' problem the group now sets about solving it. First they list all the possible causes for this problem; all the reasons why a pile of stones does not sing in tune, or why an octopus has difficulty gathering in gold dust. The reasons do not have to be realistic – after all, the problem itself is no longer realistic. The more crazy they are, the more free the mind will become of the shackles of the original problem. 'Never had singing lessons', 'crushed voice-boxes', 'fear of looking foolish' and 'being stone deaf' are all 'good' reasons why a pile of rocks cannot sing in tune. A good-humoured and relaxed group will usually come up with over a hundred 'good' reasons for the fictitious problem.

The more humour there is at this stage the better. It is not unusual for a group to be doubled up in laughter for an hour or more as they become progressively looser in their thinking, coming up with funnier and funnier analyses of the problem. People often remark that they have never laughed so much in their lives – and sometimes have sore stomach muscles the next day to prove it (while other groups in the same hotel or training centre wonder what can be so funny about a creative thinking seminar).

115

CRAZY SOLUTIONS TO A CRAZY PROBLEM

Having listed all possible causes, the group then takes each one and tries to find one or more solutions to it. In order to help deaf rocks hear, for example, they might be fitted with high-powered hearing aids. Or, to overcome their fear of looking foolish, they might first be polished. Again humour is crucial; becoming too serious only limits the number of possible solutions the group will come up with.

By the time this phase is finished – which can often take an hour or two – participants have usually become so involved in the fictitious problem that the real problem is far from their minds. Sometimes they even need reminding that all this craziness and laughter has been for a purpose; to find new approaches to the original problem.

TRIGGERS TO THE REAL PROBLEM

The next stage is to use these solutions of the fictitious problem to trigger ideas for the real problem. Thus fitting the rocks with hearing aids may trigger the idea that the desktop computers be linked through a communications package, or that they all use the same design software, or that the director should seek clearer ways of expressing his intentions. The idea of polishing the rocks may lead to the suggestion that the team should attend an interpersonal skills training, or identify and smooth out conflicts between individuals, or highlight the unique qualities and talents of each member so that they can be utilized for the team as a whole. What is important at this stage is not to translate the fictitious solutions back directly into possible real solutions, but to mentally savour each one and see what new insights they trigger.

TESTING THE NEW IDEAS

Finally, having listed all the possible solutions to the real problem, the group moves into the working out phase of the creative process. Now, at last, is the time to discard all those which clearly have no hope of success; to keep on hold those which may be worth looking into further; and to identify those which look as if they could offer potential solutions. There may be anything from five to twenty ideas which are left in this latter category, and of these three-quarters may be ideas which would have been arrived at by ordinary problem-solving approaches.

The value gained from this approach is in the other ideas which never would have been thought of. This happens because such processes encourage us to let our unconscious minds come through, and also ensure that we do not let our mindsets block our thinking.

The more lightly that we take our mindsets, the less our thinking is conditioned by the past, and the more we are able to appreciate the real magic of seeing through new eyes. This applies not just to solving problems, but to the creative management of the whole of our lives.

As we free ourselves we begin to realize that there are many other areas of challenge where we continue to live out of the past. The way we react to change can itself create unnecessary burdens and barriers to our creativity.

Chapter 6   CREATIVITY IN STRESS

My life is in the hands of any rascal who chooses to annoy
or tease me.

                              Dr John Hunter (c. 1790)

People are disturbed, not by things, but by the view they
take of them.

                              Epictetus (1st century AD)

Our creativity is clearly related to our mental state. A mind that
is rested, alive, alert, questioning and receptive is usually more
creative than a mind that is tired, tense, depressed, anxious and
resigned. Facilitating our creative flow is, therefore, also a matter
of taking care of our own state of mind and inner well-being.

The most common, and probably the most serious, impedi-
ment to a creative state of mind is too much pressure and the
stress that results. Pressure and stimulus may often be helpful in
the phase of preparation, and sometimes in implementation, but
the more intangible processes of incubation and insight are times
when we want to take the pressure off in order to allow our inner
knowing to come through.

In this there is a sad irony. The very situations in which we most need to draw upon our creative resources are frequently those situations where we experience pressure. These may be the pressures of deadlines, of responsibilities, of other people's expectations, financial worries, domestic problems or the difficulties of coping with a young family. Whatever their cause, their effect is usually one of making us feel fatigued and dull rather than relaxed and open. As a result our creativity suffers just when we need it most.

The same is true on a much wider scale. The constant acceleration in the pace of change puts us under ever greater pressure to make quick decisions, often leading us to react from old mindsets. There seems to be no time for creativity – and in the very moments when we should be stepping back to draw as fully as possible upon our creative potential.

If we are to meet the challenges facing us – as individuals, as organizations and as a species – it is therefore imperative that we not only learn how to manage our own creative processes, but also learn how to cope with increasing pressure and the stress it creates. To put it more bluntly, the art of stress management is going to become essential to our survival.

STRESS – DANGER AND OPPORTUNITY

Already the cost and consequences of stress are inestimable. As well as hindering our creativity, it has a profound impact on our health. Doctors have estimated that between 50 and 75 per cent of health problems are either caused by stress or significantly exacerbated by it. Many would put the figure even higher. A simple viral infection like a common cold may not at first sight seem to be related to stress. But it is now known that stress can damage the immune system. Thus, whether or not a virus can establish itself may be directly related to stress.

Stress also affects our vitality, our life expectancy, our relationships, our ability to listen and empathize, our openness to others, our physical stamina, our perception, our emotional stability, our tendency to error and our proneness to accidents. There is hardly an area of life which does not feel its impact, nor any person who is unaffected in some way or other. Stress is very much the epidemic of our times.

Although stress is a grave threat, it also contains a hidden opportunity. As we come to understand the inner mechanisms of our reactions to pressure, we shall see that stress is another symptom of a more general underlying issue – inappropriate mindsets, expectations and assumptions. Thus stress also offers us a doorway into our inner worlds. We can begin to see more clearly how our well-being comes to be at the mercy of the way we think and the way we see things. As we discover more about these inner dynamics, we can learn how to exercise greater choice in our responses, thus becoming the masters of our mindsets. In addition to helping maintain a healthier state of body and mind, managing our stress can also lead to a fuller appreciation of our inner natures, helping us free our own resources and respond to change more flexibly.

STRESS AND PRESSURE

The subject of stress management frequently prompts the question: Is not some stress useful? Stress can make us more dynamic; it can keep us on our toes; it can focus the mind; and it can bring mental, emotional and physical tone to our lives. Without stress would we not all be dull and flacid?

Although the question sounds simple, people differ considerably in their answers. Some agree very much with such sentiments, others feel that any stress is harmful. These differences are partly caused by the fact that the word 'stress' is not clearly defined as far as human beings are concerned. The term has been borrowed from physics, where stress is clearly defined as 'the external pressure applied to an object'. The resultant change in the object is called 'strain'. Thus the push you exert on a plank of wood is the stress; the amount it bends is the strain. When we apply the word to people, however, we mix the two terms up. We use 'stress' to refer both to the pressures we are under and to the effects it has on us.

In asking whether or not some stress is valuable, we are really asking whether or not some pressure is valuable. The answer to this is 'Yes'. If we did not have the pressure of deadlines, the pressure of other people's demands and expectations, the pressure of change, or the pressure of our own motivations and standards, we would not accomplish nearly so much. We all need stress in the sense of pressure. What we do not need is that our health, vitality and creativity should suffer as a result – that is, we do not need the 'strain'.

This approach to stress can be summarized in the simple model shown in Figure 6.1. If the demands that we are subject to are low, there may be no noticeable strain. As they increase a critical point is reached, beyond which we begin to experience some unwelcome side-effects. It is then that we begin to feel we are suffering from 'stress'.

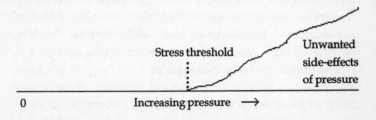

Figure 6.1

This stress threshold varies from person to person. What for one person is a demand that can be easily handled, may for another produce many unwanted side-effects. The threshold also varies within each individual. What at one time may be experienced as severe stress, may at another time, or in other circumstances, be simply mild pressure with no side-effects.

Thus the challenge we each face is how to function under pressure, without experiencing unwelcome side-effects in our thinking, our feelings, our behaviour and our bodies. How can we stay below (or not too far above) our personal threshold, and also keep this threshold as high as possible?

THE STRESS REACTION

Before exploring how we might better manage ourselves, we should first look at the 'stress reaction' itself, and at the mechanisms through which pressures can lead to these various unwanted side-effects. Of the various models that have been used to understand this reaction, the one that we feel is most useful, and best illustrates the inner processes at work, is a five-stage model. This is summarized below, and in Figure 6.2.

The demands which set the reaction off can come from many different situations. They include rush hour traffic, travel, noise, loss of job, a new job, feeling criticized, government bureaucracy, time pressures, too much responsibility, too little authority, overwork, underemployment, loud music, personal finances, moving house, a new spouse, divorce, bringing up children, family illness or death, holidays, hunger, fatigue, insomnia, interruptions, interpersonal conflicts, thwarted expectations, being stuck on a problem or feeling out of control. In short, almost anything can appear to cause stress.

But why are such situations stressful? You may, for example,

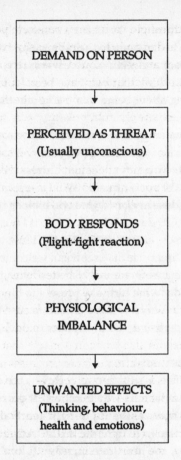

DEMAND ON PERSON

↓

PERCEIVED AS THREAT
(Usually unconscious)

↓

BODY RESPONDS
(Flight-fight reaction)

↓

PHYSIOLOGICAL
IMBALANCE

↓

UNWANTED EFFECTS
(Thinking, behaviour,
health and emotions)

Figure 6.2. Schematic model of stress reaction

be one of those people who find themselves becoming stressed
when stuck in a traffic jam. Why is this? In some respects you are
in the type of situation you have probably been longing for all
day. The phone is not ringing, there are no people bursting in
with problems to be solved, no papers to be processed, no

meetings to sit through. You have a comfortable seat, can play music of your choice, listen to the radio, adjust the temperature to suit you, sit back and relax. You are warm, dry, alone at last and with the time to think that you have been looking for all day. There is nothing about being in a traffic jam that is physically stressful.

The reason you may find it stressful is because you perceive this situation as a potential threat to your welfare, as something which may cause you difficulties and distress. What will happen if I fail to make the appointment? Will I lose face? Will I lose the contract? Will I lose my job? What will happen if I get home late for my child's birthday? What will I do if I miss the plane?

Another person, sitting in exactly the same traffic jam, may experience no threat. He may see it as a welcome opportunity to relax, take some time for himself, dictate a letter, think a problem through, consider what birthday present to buy his child, or he might even be relieved to have a good excuse for missing the plane. Such a person does not experience the jam as stressful.

THE FLIGHT-FIGHT REACTION

Once we perceive a situation as a threat, the body responds automatically in the only way it knows. It prepares for instant action. This is known as the 'flight-fight' reaction. The body gets ready either to flee or to fight the threat. Adrenalin is pumped round the body, the heart rate increases, blood pressure rises, breathing quickens, the muscles tense, the skin sweats, sugars are released into the blood to supply more energy, and the senses go on full alert.

Such a reaction would be very appropriate if we were about to be run down by a bus or attacked by a mad dog. We would need to move instantly and fast. However, most of the threats we experience are not physical threats requiring quick action. They are psychological threats requiring little or no immediate physical action. Nevertheless the same flight-fight response is triggered. We can find our hearts thumping, our palms sweating and our muscles tensing simply because someone has offended us, we have to introduce a speaker at the local club, our secretary has called in sick, or the stock market has dropped again.

The body has prepared us to 'run for our life' or 'fight to the death'. But in almost every circumstance in which the reaction is triggered, such a response is neither appropriate nor desirable. In other words, there has been a false alarm. So, while we get on with our day, the body has to recover and regain its normal state. This may take anything from minutes to hours, depending on the intensity of the reaction.

If such unnecessary reactions occurred only occasionally they would not present a major problem. Many of us, however, do not have time to recover from one dose of the flight-fight reaction before the next one sets in. When this pattern is repeated several times a day the body ends up in a permanent state of emergency – although most of the time there is no emergency at all.

It is this that makes stress such a danger to health. Virtually every organ in the body is influenced by this response. When it continues month after month, our physical systems naturally become strained, and eventually malfunction.

Moreover, there is an unfortunate vicious circle at work. The more stressed we become, the more vulnerable we become to stress. The weaker our system, the lower our stress threshold becomes. What previously would have been tolerable pressure becomes an intolerable burden, and in the extreme can lead to breakdown. It is this that leads the sane and rational manager to sack her secretary because the coffee is cold!

EARLY WARNING SIGNS

Clearly, if we are to manage our reactions to increasing pressure successfully, we cannot afford to wait for such serious signs of stress to appear. We need to catch the indications of not being able to cope with pressure as soon as possible. The various symptoms of strain are many and diverse, but spotted early they can be valuable signals that we have passed our personal stress threshold.

• In our bodies we may experience symptoms such as headaches, indigestion, a throbbing heart, breathlessness, frequent colds or the recurrence of previous infections, susceptibility to allergies, excessive sweating, clenched fists, tight jaw, fainting, twitching muscles, nausea, tiredness, constipation or diarrhoea, vague aches and pains, rapid gain or loss in weight, skin rashes and irritations.

• Mentally we may find ourselves thinking less clearly, becoming indecisive, making mistakes, forgetful, less intuitive, losing concentration, easily distracted, less sensitive, having persistent negative thoughts and bad dreams or nightmares, focusing on short-term thinking, worrying more or making hasty decisions.

• Emotionally we may experience irritability, anger, alienation, mild paranoias, nervousness, apprehensiveness, gloom, depression, anxiety, fussiness, pointlessness, loss of confidence, tension, decreasing satisfaction, meaninglessness, feeling drained, lack of enthusiasm, demotivation, feeling attacked, low self-esteem, cynicism, inappropriate humour or job dissatisfaction.

• In our behaviour we may notice ourselves feeling unsociable, restless, unable to unwind, losing our appetite or overeating, achieving less, losing interest in sex (or overindulging), becoming accident-prone, sleeping badly or unable to go to sleep, sleeping too much, driving badly, lying, drinking more alcohol, smoking more, muddling our words, taking work home more, too busy to relax, unable to manage time well, not looking after ourselves, withdrawing from supportive relationships, or experiencing increased problems at home.

Individually, any of these symptoms would not merit much attention, and we might easily dismiss them. Together they can present us with a good picture of our overall well-being. A fairly healthy person, coping adequately with the pressures of life, may experience between five and ten of these signs. If you are scoring between ten and twenty, the pressure is obviously beginning to result in more than a healthy number of side-effects. If you are scoring even higher, you probably need to take your body's gentle warnings very seriously.

One young and ambitious manager in a research department totalled over forty on the above lists. As with most people who score high, he knew what was causing him so much stress. In his case it was the uncomfortable relationship that had developed with his boss, particularly the fact that neither of them had brought the issue out into the open. He felt trapped, unable to resolve the situation, and resigned to a difficult work environment.

Three months later, on counting up the number of early warning signs again, he found his score had increased another five points. As one might imagine, this frightened him. It also shocked him into taking responsibility for changing the situation. After facing the issue with his boss, he managed to arrange a transfer to another division where he knew there would be support. Six months later his score had come down to below thirty – still high, but improving.

These signals had not only helped him tackle this particular conflict at work, they had also made him realize that there were deeper personal issues he needed to deal with – his own attitude to authority and relationships, his feeling of self-worth and his sense of purpose. Using this opportunity, he spent time working with himself, and over the next two years came to terms with these issues.

Keeping a regular eye on these early warning signs is a useful way of monitoring your own reactions to the pressures you are under – especially as the pressures increase. The list above can be used to take your 'stress temperature' every month or so. Notice what your normal score appears to be, and pay particular attention when it begins to increase. You might also note in which category you experience the most symptoms. This will vary from person to person, and shows in which area of your life you are most likely to see the impact of stress.

STRESS AND OUR ATTITUDE TO LIFE

Although we know a lot about the physiology of stress, and the effects it has upon our lives, we are only just beginning to become aware of the role which our thoughts and feelings play in the creation of stress. One area in which this relationship is becoming very apparent is in our health, particularly in the health of our hearts. James Lynch, author of *The Broken Heart*, writes in his more recent book, *The Language of the Heart*:

Medical statistics on the loss of human companionship, the lack of love, and human loneliness quickly revealed that the expression *broken heart* is not just a poetic image for loneliness and despair but is an overwhelming medical reality. All the available data pointed to the lack of human companionship, chronic loneliness, social isolation, and the sudden loss of a loved one as being among the leading causes of premature death in the United States. And while we found that the effects of human loneliness were related to virtually every major disease – whether cancer, pneumonia, or mental disease – they were particularly apparent in heart disease.

Another factor which appears to affect heart disease is our general approach to life. Nearly thirty years ago two cardiologists, Meyer Friedman and Ray Rosenman coined the term 'A-type' personality to describe the sort of person who was always trying to do more, and faster. A-types are concerned with speed, performance and productivity. They tend to be aggressive, impatient, intolerant, hard driving and always hurried. They are also, it was discovered, much more likely to have heart attacks.

Underlying this behaviour is a pattern of attitudes. A-type people tend to be preoccupied with time. They are eager to get started, eager to finish, never willing to waste time and have an aversion to queueing. They also show a strong competitive tendency, setting high standards for themselves, always wanting to succeed and be seen to be doing well. In short, they are preoccupied with efficiency, involved in a chronic, incessant struggle to achieve more and more in less and less time.

Such attitudes are not all bad. The world today needs people who are efficient, strive for excellence, thrive on competition and make sure that things get done on time. The problem arises when these attitudes get out of balance. The A-type person becomes a victim of these traits and lets them rule areas of his life where they are inappropriate. Thus the A-type will easily become competitive when playing with his children. On holiday he will try to pack as much into each day as possible, having forgotten how to take it easy. He has become addicted to efficiency and achievement.

Looked at from a much broader perspective, the A-type pattern reflects some of the more extreme attitudes and values underlying the crisis in which humanity as a whole finds itself. This, we have seen, is a crisis which is fuelled by an attachment to growth, a preoccupation with efficiency, a desire to be in control of the world, the deification of logic and rationality, an imbalance towards masculine values, and a reluctance to deal with emotions and the hidden dimensions of life. We could say that Western society has become an A-type society. And although we may not all be strong A-types, there are probably areas in most of our lives in which this pattern appears.

As the pace of change continues to accelerate, there are going to be increasing pressures on us all to respond faster and perform more effectively. Managing our A-type attitudes and not allowing them to take control of our lives is, therefore, going to become more and more of a necessity.

Reducing these tendencies is not, however, simply a matter of modifying behaviour. People quickly find this does not last. If we are to avoid this trap we must explore and modify the attitudes and inner values which underlie these behaviour patterns. A good way of doing this is to ask ourselves some simple, but often quite penetrating, questions that can help us step back from the mindsets which perpetuate the A-type attitude, and take a fresh look at life.

What do I really want?

Why am I doing this?

What is the most important thing to me?

What is my dream for life?

What is time for?

Is this really so urgent?

What's the worst that could happen?

Will any of this matter in ten years' time?

How would I look at this if I had only six months to live?

AVOIDING BREAKDOWN

Some people are fortunate in that they can choose to step back before the effects of stress take hold and the vicious circle winds up. Others are not so lucky. They have become so firmly caught in its grasp they are unable to help themselves.

In England a senior civil servant, working in the National Health Service, had been struggling for ten years to provide a high level of patient care with decreasing manpower, reduced budgets and an increasingly demotivated staff, while at the same time having to battle with a senior management which did not share the same values. Others might have given up and taken a senior position in the private sector, but this was not on his list of options. He was very committed to his staff and to doing a thorough professional job, and devoted to helping other people. To compound his difficulties, he was faced with personal problems. He was feeling increasingly lonely, yet so drained that he had no time for social activities. He became a workaholic, and more isolated.

About five years ago he realized that he had to do something about his situation. He tried taking long holidays in order to relieve the pressure, only to find himself returning to an increasing workload. He restructured the responsibilities throughout his division, but that only resulted in more interpersonal problems. He attended a number of senior management courses in an attempt to learn new skills to deal with the crisis. But still his problems continued.

Throughout this period he was perceived to be managing well, and was even offered a number of promotions with additional responsibilities. Outwardly everything seemed fine; but inwardly there was increasing turmoil and panic. Nothing he did seemed to relieve the pressure.

After two more years he broke down. He had a minor heart attack, and was finally forced to admit he could no longer cope. Over the next few months, as he began to step back and look at what he had been doing, he slowly began to realize that the real changes he needed to make were inner changes rather than outer changes – changes in his attitudes and his approach to life as a whole.

FROM FATIGUE TO EXHAUSTION

Peter Nixon, a London cardiologist who has spent many years studying the effect of increasing pressure on human performance, has developed a picture of the route people take through fatigue and exhaustion to the edge of breakdown.

In healthy fatigue a person recognizes they are tired as a result of working hard or lack of sleep, and can redress the balance with one or two good nights' sleep. However, when people who are already fatigued face additional demands, they often assume that they can accommodate these extra pressures by pushing themselves a little bit harder. If they are not yet at the top of their curve then performance may well increase. But if their performance is already at its maximum, then, rather than continuing as expected in the direction of the dotted line in Figure 6.3, they find

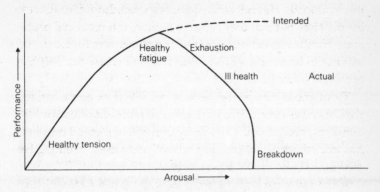

Figure 6.3. Peter Nixon's 'Human function curve'.

their performance now goes down.

Such people enter the vicious circle of exhaustion. They become increasingly tired, their performance decreases further, they push themselves even harder, and become even more exhausted. They become angry and despairing as they find themselves caught in a trap from which they can see no way out. They know all is not well, but they see the cause of their suffering in the world around them and other people. Victims to their condition they find it almost impossible to take any steps to help themselves.

If the additional demands are short-lived the person may return to healthy fatigue. If they are maintained the person's well-being steadily deteriorates, leading over the years to ill-health and eventual breakdown.

Nixon has found that the first and crucial step before any treatment can begin is a period of prolonged sleep – often for fifteen hours a day for several days. Only then are these people ready to step back and recognize the underlying attitudes and beliefs that have brought about this extreme condition, and begin the slow process of taking a fresh look at themselves and their lives.

Although you almost certainly are not in this state -- if you were, you would not have the time to be reading this -- there are learnings for us all in this pattern. We need to recognize our own levels of fatigue and take time to rest, rather than be laid out for weeks when exhaustion does set in. The faster our lives become the more important this will be. If we allow ourselves to be ruled by the increasing speed around us, we will become more and more fatigued. If we are to preserve an inner alertness and stability we must balance our activity with rest. Yet the very times we need rest are often the times when it seems that we can least afford to take it. But if we do not keep this inner balance and freshness, we have little hope of becoming more creative. We will be more likely to drown in change.

IS IT ALL IN THE MIND?

Maintaining inner stability is also a question of how we choose to see things. As with the case of a traffic jam, the same situation can cause a marked stress reaction in one person and very little reaction in another. Clearly, whether or not we experience stress depends partly on the situation and partly on how we see it. If we see what is happening as a potential threat to our well-being, then we trigger a stress reaction. Yet, because this aspect of the process is largely unconscious, it is often overlooked, and we think it is the external demand alone which is the cause of our suffering. This is why the second step in the model in Figure 6.2 is so important. It sheds more light on the inner mechanisms which lie behind much of our apparent stress.

The 'cause' of many of our stressful reactions is a combination of the situation we are in and the way we perceive it. When we perceive a conflict between the way things are and how we believe they should be, we may, if too attached to our belief, begin to feel threatened. It is our inability to handle this inner conflict which lies at the heart of so much of our stress.

Imagine, for example, you are in a meeting and are interrupted by a phone call from your wife. She has called with good news: your daughter has passed her exams. If you believe this is something worth being interrupted for, you will be both pleased that she called, and pleased with her news. If, on the other hand, you believe that she should not phone you during work hours except in dire emergencies, you may feel irritated, and not even be able to hear her good news. There is a conflict between what is (her calling) and what you think should be (her not calling).

You may be trying to catch an international flight, and arrive twenty-five minutes before take-off, only to be told that the latest check-in time was thirty minutes before departure. You can see in the lounge in front of you that boarding has not yet begun, but you are told that the desk is closed, and 'rules are rules'. In such circumstances most of us feel upset, to say the least. Our mindset is that we should be allowed on. The reality is different. 'What is' and 'what should be' are again in conflict; and we become distressed.

Or, suppose you are finding it difficult to go to sleep. You are in a warm bed, well fed and ready for eight hours sleep, but sleep is not forthcoming. The voice in your head tells you that you should be able to sleep; but you cannot. The more this continues, the more tension you create – and the less likely you are to sleep. Again our perception of the situation determines our reaction.

As can be seen in Figure 6.4, the underlying mechanism of such conflicts closely parallels the fundamental mechanism of mindsets that we explored in Chapter 4. The incoming sensory data is in itself neutral, and without meaning. It is only in matching it with past experience that we create a particular perception and meaning. Similarly with much of our stress, the situations we find ourselves in are, in themselves, neutral. They take on significance when we try to match them with our expectations and mindsets as to how things should be. If this results in conflict, we create stress for ourselves.

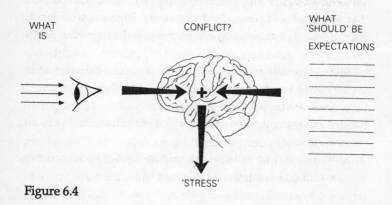

WHAT IS   CONFLICT?   WHAT 'SHOULD' BE

EXPECTATIONS

'STRESS'

Figure 6.4

Stress is also created when the situations we are in conflict with our deeper needs and values. If, when your wife phones during a meeting, you imagine that the other people you are with will disapprove of her calling you, then the threat is exacerbated. There is now an additional conflict between 'what is' and your need for approval.

If the mortgage rate goes up – or even if we fear it will – our need for security may be threatened. The possibility of losing our job is almost certain to trigger stress – not only security is at stake here, but also our self-esteem. Flying is stressful for some people because their sense of being in control is seriously threatened. Driving a car is statistically far less safe than flying, but at least we feel more in control. We may be doing an undemanding job, and yet experience considerable stress because our need for creative expression is continually thwarted. Many of us may find ourselves stressed by the horrors of child abuse. Neither us nor our children may be directly threatened, but some of our deepest values are.

Again, it is not just the external situation that is causing the stress (although it often seems that way); it is the conflict between the situation and our judgement of it. This process and its consequences can be summarized in the following four points.

- A stressful reaction is something we create in ourselves.
- It is our perception of events, rather than the events themselves, which is the problem.
- Believing it is the events which are responsible keeps us a victim.
- You, and no one else, are responsible for your reactions, emotional, mental and physical.

For many people this hidden side of our creative ability can come as a surprise. But it can also be a revelation and a release. As we become more conscious of these inner dynamics, we can take greater responsibility for them, and in doing so open to ourselves a new way of managing stress.

MANAGING OUR REACTIONS

Most approaches to stress management focus on managing the external causes of stress and on managing the effects it has on us. If our production assistant is always late, resulting in considerable inconvenience and stress, we can remove the 'cause' by removing the person who is to blame. If time pressures are a problem, we can ease the load by practising better time management. Or if greasy food stresses our liver, we may remedy this by changing our diet.

If the effect of stress is to make us exhausted, we can take more sleep or practise some relaxation or meditation technique. If the effect is that we are continually wound up, we may find that exercise such as jogging, swimming, squash or even walking helps us wind down. If stress means we bottle up emotions, finding someone who is willing to listen to us without judgement can help us get these feelings off our chest.

While such approaches certainly help, they do not get to the root of the problem. As we have seen, stress is more than a simple cause-effect reaction. The inner dimension of this process – our perceptions, expectations, beliefs and needs – are also a central element in the equation. This opens up to us another way of handling stress.

When caught in a traffic jam, for example, rather than seeing it as a threat and wishing it would go away, we could ask ourselves, 'What is the opportunity here?' 'What is the best use I can make of this time?' By doing so we would probably experience a very different set of reactions. Maybe we would still be late, but we would be considerably less stressed.

Simple questions can again be useful in discovering what is really going on inside us. The next time you feel upset by someone or something, you might like to stop for a moment and ask yourself:

What am I telling myself that is making me feel this way?
What is the expectation I have that is being challenged in this situation?
Am I demanding that I should be treated in a particular way?

What am I assuming about what I need to be happy?
Am I blaming another for disturbing my peace of mind
when really it is only my judgements that are disturbing
me?
What is really being threatened?

When we are under a lot of pressure we often find it very
difficult to handle our emotions. When we are angry at someone
for not behaving as we would like, it is very easy to place all the
blame for our distress on the other person. 'After all,' we say to
ourselves, 'if he had not behaved as he did, I would not be so
upset.' But equally, if we had not been so attached to our
expectations and projected them on to the other person, we
would not have felt so threatened by his behaviour, and the
conflict inside us would not have escalated.

If we find ourselves angry in such a situation, we can defuse
our reaction by stopping for a moment and asking ourselves,
'What might he have been thinking?' 'How might he have been
feeling in this situation?' 'What past experiences could have led
him to behave this way?' 'What might he have been hoping to
achieve?' This is not to make the other person's behaviour right,
nor to deny our own values. But if we can step back in this way,
we may see his behaviour from another perspective – and maybe
find that as well as our anger there is also compassion.

THE WAY OF THE CREATIVE MANAGER WITH STRESS

We have said before that the way of the creative manager is an
inner way. He recognizes that, as well as taking care of the outer
aspects of change, we also have to handle its inner dimensions –
the attitudes, perceptions and values that lead us to respond in
the ways we do. This is also the way the creative manager copes

with increasing pressures in life. As well as tending to the more tangible sides of stress, he also tends to the inner processes behind our reactions.

In this respect stress resembles the frustration phase of the creative process. If we only see frustration as a barrier to be pushed past, we may prevent ourselves from hearing what it is trying to tell us, and the frustration will in all likelihood continue. If, on the other hand, frustration is seen as an opportunity – a call to step back and listen to our own inner voice – we can move beyond it and draw more deeply upon our creativity.

Similarly, if stress is seen only as a barrier to our functioning, we will tend to manage only its outer forms, its causes and effects. If we see it as an opportunity to learn more about our own selves, and what is really important to us, it can become another window into ourselves. It is a signal that there is more to learn about our inner worlds.

In seeking to manage the beliefs and expectations that lie behind stress, we are taking another step in freeing ourselves from our inner limitations. We are creating the opportunity to be more at peace with ourselves. Rather than being tossed around by the seas of change, we can learn to ride them with greater inner calm. As we have seen, such stability is going to become critical to our ability to handle increasing change. If we can remain calm within, and more open to our selves, we will be able to think and act with greater clarity, creativity and humanity.

Learning to manage our reactions to pressure is part of the daily practice of the creative manager, for, in learning to handle these hidden aspects of stress, we are also learning to bridge our inner and outer worlds. It is learning to think about life in a new way. And this is the essence of humanity's task today.

Chapter 7   SOCIAL RE-CREATION

> There is no need to run outside
> For better seeing,
> Nor to peer from a window. Rather abide
> At the centre of your being;
> For the more you leave it, the less you learn.
> Search your heart and see
> If he is wise who takes each turn:
> The way to do is to be.
>
> Lao-Tze (6th century BC)

Clearly the twenty-first century will place radically different and unprecedented demands on us all. While many of the creators and managers of organizations – whether they be large or small, governmental or commercial, profit or non-profit – will bear a particular responsibility for navigating humanity through these turbulent times, the challenge will be one we will all have to confront.

Where will we go for help? Will we, like our parents, believe that by turning to experts such as scientists, engineers, politicians and corporate leaders, we will be able to control change and cope with the waves breaking over us? Many of us know in our hearts that this strategy no longer works. We are going to need help of a different order.

As we have begun to see in previous chapters, the basic blocks to change are on the inside rather than the outside. The more we understand ourselves, the more we can see what lies behind our fears, both conscious and unconscious. As we come to see them in a different light, we become more free and willing to change. Learning about our selves thus becomes a central focus in the life of the creative manager.

THE WAY OF LEARNING

For most people learning is synonymous with education. We spend anything from twelve to twenty years of our lives in schools and colleges, learning for the life ahead. We may then assume that our formal education is finished. But we also recognize that this education only partially equips us for life today.

Many of our current educational systems are based on the need to train people for a society rooted in the Industrial Revolution. Then it was important to give large numbers of people the skills and techniques appropriate to the tasks of that age. Life-long skills were required for lifelong tasks.

Today, and in the years to come, we need learning that is relevant to the challenges of the Information Age. First, the speed of change demands that learning should be continuous and lifelong. And second, there are new, inner skills we need to learn.

Many of the more exciting new developments in learning are taking place within organizations. Faced with the pressing need to develop personal skills such as thinking and planning, leadership, communication, working in groups, and creativity, in addition to the many new information-technology skills, organizations have taken over much of the task of continuing education. Some have established their own education centres and colleges. Many support their employees in on-going education programmes outside the company. Traditional training departments are rapidly changing their focus from specific job skills to a more general education of the person as a whole. The more leading edge the company, the greater the emphasis on continuous learning; some even require their managers to attend at least two weeks of education every year.

This increasing awareness of a new attitude to learning is reflected in a comment from one of the captains of industry interviewed by Francis Kinsman. Speaking of the changes which will come in the 1990s, he emphasized,

> The most serious impact will fall upon those who have given up learning. For them, adopting different attitudes will be a difficult and painful process.
>
> In industry this particularly applies to the middle-aged managers.

This does not imply that all have given up. Many are indeed taking a fresh look at their own learning. As the managing director of a large construction corporation discovered,

> I have realised that even though I am 48 years old I can actually open myself to learn. I thought I had stopped when I finished school, but now I can begin again.

In the future we will need radically different personal skills and attitudes. In the past we tended to assume that to change the world it was sufficient to change our behaviour, and to learn new and better techniques of control. Consequently, we have learnt to organize and manage the outer forms of our personal and professional lives. We have learnt how to read balance sheets, how to set up new companies, how to produce and market new products, how to co-ordinate international operations, how to use and implement new technology, and how to design and stage elaborate events. Yet, although we may know much concerning the world around us and how to control it, we are also recognizing that focusing on the outer alone does not necessarily help us cope better with the more personal aspects of change. On the contrary, if we continue to react only to its external aspects we run the risk of breakdown, both individually and socially.

Historically, education and teaching have largely depended on the outer expert. Today, however, there is increasing recognition that learning is a process that takes place from within the person, and that we need to invest the same energy and commitment we already make to outer development into exploring our inner worlds.

RE-VISIONING SELF-EXPLORATION AND SELF-DISCOVERY

Most people only consider the idea of self-exploration and inner discovery when there is a problem. So much so that until recently inner guidance has been regarded as the province of the therapist, the psychiatrist, and the priest. Over the last two decades, however, there has been an explosion of interest in self-development – almost as rapid as the explosion of information technology. But, being a far less tangible phenomenon, its impact is not at first so visible.

Willis Harman regards this 'human potential movement' as a new science of subjective experience with profound implications for our future. He summarizes the basic tenets of this changing image of the person in three propositions:

• The potentialities of the individual human being are far greater than currently in-vogue models of man would lead us to think possible.

• A far greater proportion of significant human experience than we ordinarily assume is comprised of unconscious processes . . . It includes those mysterious realms of experience we refer to as 'intuition' and 'creativity'.

• Included in these partly or largely unconscious processes are images of the self and limitations of the self, and images of the future, which play a predominant role in limiting or enhancing actualization of one's capacities.

He goes on to comment that,
we have undersold man, underestimated his possibilities, and misunderstood what is needed for what Boulding terms 'the great Transition'. [These tenets] imply that the most profound revolution of the educational system would not be the cybernation of knowledge transmission, but the infusion of an exalted image of what man can be and the cultivation of an enhanced self image in each individual child.

It is this other dimension of learning that is so crucial to the present times, and the various paths of the human potential movement can be seen as pioneering ventures into this largely uncharted territory. Activities such as meditation, yoga, relaxation, biofeedback, counselling, psychotherapy, martial arts and bodywork are sometimes regarded as a symptom of the 'me' era – a narcissistic indulgence and a flight from the 'real world'. While there may be an element of truth in this, it would be a mistake to believe that this is all they are. They can also be seen as people from all walks of life responding to an inner call to understand themselves and life more fully. They are symptoms of a growing search for meaning.

CHANGING VALUES

The human potential movement is but one face of a much larger social phenomenon. Since the early 1970s it has become apparent that, throughout the more industrialized countries, individual values and motivations are steadily changing . These trends have been the subject of a number of long-term studies, including the Stanford Research Institute's Values and Lifestyles (VALS) Program, the UK Monitor Programme, the European RISC (International Research Institute into Social Change) study, the Naisbitt Group's *Trend Report*, and Yankelovich's research. They have revealed that while the majority of people may still be focused on their outer material well-being, the concern with inner values and self-direction is growing steadily, and is now a significant factor in social development. Chris and Kirk MacNulty, from the VALS and Monitor programmes, call this emerging set of values 'inner directed'.

> Inner directed people are motivated by self-actualisation. They are largely unconcerned about the opinion of them held by the world at large; their criteria for success and the standards of their behaviour are within

themselves. This does not imply withdrawn or reclusive behaviour. Indeed the inner-directed individual usually has a broad horizon, a good understanding of world events and a high tolerance for other people's behaviour.

Daniel Yankelovich in his book *New Rules: Searching for Self-Fulfilment in a World Turned Upside Down*, finds the same trend, though he puts it slightly differently:

Americans are weighing the rewards of conventional success against less lucrative but more satisfying personal achievements and are seriously considering the latter.

Kirk MacNulty describes the emergence of an 'inner directed' population over the past thirty years as:

a natural phenomenon, the result of an evolutionary process, if you like. Like the enquiring, intellectual experimental researchers (nascent physical scientists) who emerged from the religiously orientated society of mediaeval Europe, the Inner Directed population does not appear to be the product of any of our social institutions . . . Like his scientific predecessor, the Inner Directed fits as uncomfortably into the materialism of the Industrial paradigm as Galileo fitted into the dogma of the church.

The emergence of these new values can be seen as part of a much older historical trend. For centuries, the dominant need was for sustenance and survival, and the majority of people spent their waking hours working the land. The new technology and economics of the Industrial Revolution provided the opportunity for greater material well-being and release from the drudgery of a survival driven existence.

Over the next two centuries increasing numbers of people became concerned with creating a more comfortable physical environment. Increasingly they had the means to improve sanitation, housing, clothing, food, transportation, communication, medical care, schooling and the means of producing more and more goods to facilitate these changes. This provided the platform for the emergence of a consumer driven society.

The dominating motivations shifted away from sustenance and survival towards personal security and material well-being. People became, in the language of the VALS and Monitor programmes, more 'outer-directed' in the sense that their motivations were increasingly dominated by a need to improve their social position. This has led to a society in which many are driven by the need to be seen and recognized by others – a need which often gives birth to the belief that financial and material well-being are all important.

TOWARDS AUTONOMY AND SELF-DIRECTION

Today, however, new opportunities are opening up to us and another shift in personal values is becoming apparent. It is now rapidly becoming obvious that the values of the industrial era, which regarded work, physical security, material development and economic growth as priorities, are no longer appropriate. Important as they have been for raising the quality of life and personal welfare, these very values now threaten our continued collective well-being and survival. In addition, work as we have known it is becoming redundant.

Information technology is freeing many from the drudgery of work. Robots are taking over factory production lines, computers have replaced roomfuls of account clerks, and word processing has transformed the publishing industry. Soon voice recognition and high level software will put traditional secretaries out of work; expert systems will take over much of the routine in medicine, education and scientific research; computer-generated film will put Hollywood in a briefcase; sales-driven data banks will replace marketing departments; artificial intelligence will reduce the need for lawyers, accountants, civil servants and many of the other tasks intrinsic to the industrial society. There are hardly any professions which will not be dramatically affected, if not eliminated, by the Information Revolution. At least 75 per cent of work as we know it today may well have been eliminated by the turn of the century.

To some this may seem a most undesirable state of affairs. In the short term it will clearly bring a painful disruption to many people's lives, and much will need to be done to help people through these difficult personal transitions. It will also face society as a whole with a challenge far greater than that posed by the Industrial Revolution, for it will shake the very foundations of our economic system.

One natural response is to try and hold back the tide of change and seek ways to return to full employment. We should not, however, forget that the reduction of work has been our goal for centuries. The history of the Industrial Age is the history of labour-saving devices. From the early days of steam engines, water pumps and cotton looms, we have progressed to the production of washing machines, dishwashers, vacuum cleaners, food-processors, electric can-openers, toasters, power drills, car washers, automated petrol pumps, take-away and convenience foods, electronic cash dispensers, self-drive lawn-mowers, electric golf-carts and a wealth of other equipment designed to minimize unnecessary work and free up our lives. Now, with the extraordinary and unprecedented freedoms that information technology is bringing to us, we may be approaching the point where many of us do not have to work at all.

But what is all this growing freedom for?

Faced with such a rapidly changing world in which so much of what we have held to be important is falling away, old values are beginning to wane. People are asking themselves, 'What is deeply important to me?' 'What is it I truly care about?' 'What do I really want to do with my life?' This is not just another manifestation of the selfishness that so dogs our current society; it is a fundamental re-evaluation of the values by which we live. It is about how we want to be, rather than what we want to have. It is about setting our standards rather than deriving them from what others tells us, or from how others behave. It is about being true to ourselves, rather than being over-concerned with appearances and status. This is the essence of the shift towards inner-directed values.

What is more, this is the first time in our history that it has been possible for large numbers of people to follow these inclinations. Previously it was only possible for a privileged elite. Now, having created more time for ourselves, we have the freedom to ask these fundamental questions. Furthermore, with a higher quality of life and better material well-being, we have greater opportunities to follow these inner promptings and make them a part of our daily living.

In short, we are being freed to explore our inner worlds, to develop our thinking and use our minds in a different way. Perhaps this is the real revolution – and the hidden opportunity behind the Information Age.

Chapter 8   THE INNER WORLD
OF THE CREATIVE
MANAGER

*'Trust thyself.' Every heart vibrates to that iron string. The
great have always done so. We now must accept the same
transcendent destiny.*

Ralph Waldo Emerson (1841)

As we have just seen people today are increasingly asking
themselves what it is they really want to do. For some this
questioning dawns slowly; for others it can come as a sudden
shock. It can happen both at times of great happiness and joy and
also at times of crisis and personal suffering.

We may have had the experience of suddenly being made
redundant, for example, or we may know of a friend or relative
to whom this has happened. For some this may bring deep
despair and hopelessness, leading them to some fundamental
questions about themselves and their lives.

Others may see redundancy as an opportunity to do what they
have always wanted and use their newfound freedom to involve
themselves in a life that has more meaning. There are many
examples of people who have chosen not to continue with a
business career at all, but to work in the helping professions
where they may find less pay but greater satisfaction. Others

have decided to dedicate themselves to trying to preserve the environment.

Facing death can be another crisis that brings us up against such questions. Whether it be through a heart attack, discovering we have cancer or another major illness, a serious accident, or simply coming to terms with our own mortality, our lives may be suddenly brought into sharp focus, leading us to take a fresh look at our values and priorities.

The same can happen when faced with the death or deep suffering of someone close to us. We may be moved to look at the purpose and meaning in our own lives, and reconsider the opportunity our lives present us with.

A similar personal re-evaluation can sometimes happen when we seem to be doing well. Having achieved considerable material security, professional success and personal recognition, we may, for no apparent reason, find ourselves feeling bored, frustrated, without purpose and perhaps depressed.

Our initial reaction may be to try to modify our external situation. We may try to change our 'boring and unsatisfying' work environment for a 'more interesting one', or even change our job. We may change our home for a 'better' one. Or we may think about changing our partner and seek new relationships.

More often than not, such reactions are only a way of avoiding the more disturbing questions that face us, and very little is resolved. If we are to move beyond the crisis rather than simply patch it over, we must turn inwards and face ourselves. Our frustration and discomfort should, once again, be seen as a call from within. It is the voice of our own self reminding us to listen to a deeper truth.

As we saw earlier, society is facing a very similar existential crisis. We are being obliged to challenge many assumptions, to look at the world in new ways, and to reconsider our priorities.

In this respect we are all undergoing a crisis of values. Every one of us is being asked to listen to the voice within, and to let it speak through our decisions and actions.

THE VOICE WITHIN

What is the voice within? It is the part of us which feels that something is not quite right. It is the part that tells us when we are pushing ourselves too hard. It is the recognition that we did not treat someone fairly. It is the sense that something is going on behind another's words. It is the hunch that we should hold back a while rather than rushing in.

The voice within is also that part of us that tries to tell us what is best. It is the inner knowing that tries to speak to us in our dreams. It is the intuition that leads us to call a friend at the right time. It is the feeling that there is more to life. It is the urge to follow a higher purpose.

Although this voice is within us all, and at all times, it is not always easy to hear. The clamour of the world around is so much louder. Moreover, our outer-orientated society prefers us to believe it is not real, and not to be listened to. Its counsel often goes against all that convention would have us hear.

Nor do we have many skills or techniques with which to hear our quieter intimations. Most of the skills we have learnt are skills that help us handle the world around more than the world within. They are of little value when it comes to managing our inner processes. To co-operate with the intangible we do not need techniques so much as self-understanding, self-trust, and a willingness to stop 'doing' and listen.

As was apparent from our exploration of the creative process, it is this willingness to listen to our own inner worlds that is the mark of the creative manager. We need to listen to ourselves to know at what stage we are and where we should go to next. We need to listen to our frustration to hear what it is trying to tell us. Is the voice that says, 'I can go no further,' telling us it is time to do something completely different and incubate for a while? Or is our feeling of not getting anywhere a sign that we have not done enough preparation? Only we know. There are no rules to follow in the creative process – except the rule of listening and trusting our inner voice.

Of all the phases of creativity, insight most of all demands that we respect our inner truth. It is, quite literally, an 'in-sight'; a time when we suddenly 'see' a new connection, a new way through. The whole of the creative process is centred around this moment when our deeper knowing breaks through. Kekulé already knew the answer to the problem of the benzene structure; but he needed to turn off his questing mind, relax and float in dreams before his subconscious could speak to him.

None of this is to imply that the inner voice is always right. Like any aspect of our mind, it can be fallible. This is why testing and evaluating is also a crucial part of creativity. The value of learning to listen to this inner sense is not to arrive at incontrovertible truth, but to open ourselves to another aspect of ourselves beyond our normal thinking. And when we do, we often find that this deeper guidance contains a wisdom that our conscious thinking was unable to reveal.

VALUING OUR IMAGINATION

In order to understand our inner tuitions, we need first to recognize the different languages of the mind. Seldom do the deeper levels of the mind speak to us in words. The deeper levels of the mind are much happier communicating in images, sensations, dreams and feelings.

This is partly because verbal language is, from an evolutionary perspective, relatively new to the human brain. Sensory imagery, on the other hand, is much older and more fundamental. As a result most of us remember sounds, smells and sights, more easily than phrases or sentences. The smell of new-baked bread transports us to the farmhouse kitchen of our childhood. We dream in pictures rather than words. When we think of tomorrow it is usually images that come to mind. We may have warm feelings as we imagine the reception awaiting us as we return home from a long trip. We may sense our hunches in our body. Even as you read these examples, your mind was very probably turning them into images of one form or another.

Such imagery may not always be vivid or photographic. Nor need it be only visual; the other senses can speak to us just as clearly. Yet in one form or another imagery is nearly always in our minds.

(If you believe you are a person who does not easily create images, then, whatever happens, do not now imagine a green door – anything else but a green door! Or the sound of someone knocking on it!)

To hear our inner voice, we should, therefore, listen in the languages that the mind uses to speak to itself, rather than the language that we use to communicate with other people. One helpful way of doing this is to symbolize our inner knowing as a wise person.

Sometime when you have half an hour to yourself, find a quiet place where you will not be disturbed, settle down, close your eyes, and take some minutes to relax. Then imagine yourself in a garden, allowing images to float into your mind, however they may come, listening to sounds, imagining textures, as well as watching any visual images. After a few more minutes, imagine that you see a wise person coming towards you. Again allow the images of this person to come freely; do not try and force the person to look or be any particular way.

Having become acquainted with this wise person, you might try asking questions on subjects where you would like some guidance. Listen to what he or she has to tell you. Maybe they have something to show you – again words are not always the most appropriate form of communication. Alternatively, you may just ask this person if there is anything else they would like to bring to your attention. The answers may be surprising; but often they are just what we need. They are what we need to tell ourselves, but could not hear until we gave our inner voice a symbolic form.

Another important value of imagery is its ability to take us beyond our crystallized mindsets. For this reason many organizations are beginning to use images as a way of seeing past the outdated, mechanistic and one-dimensional systems-view that have shaped their corporate cultures. In his ground-breaking book *Images of the Organization* Gareth Morgan shows how organizations of the past are often described in images of machines, while images of brains and brain processes, or trees with their branch and root systems, can be used as metaphors which evoke a more alive and creative view of the organization and the complex issues it is faced with.

MINDSETS AND INNER NEEDS

Our mindsets about what should or should not be, or about how we should or should not behave, can often stand in the way of our hearing our deeper knowing. Earlier we saw how they can blinker our thinking and creativity by leading us to make false assumptions; and that by holding on to them, we may see threats that do not really exist, and so limit our creative response to pressure. We have also seen the unconscious influence they exert on the value systems that characterize an age. Yet mindsets are also very necessary; without them we would not be able to evaluate and give meaning to the world.

Our approach so far has been one of accepting our mindsets. This is not to make them right or wrong, but by acknowledging them, and the role they play in our thinking and perception, we can take greater responsibility for the effects they have on our decisions and behaviour. Sometimes, however, we may become aware of mindsets that are inappropriate, and that we would like to change or be without. What do we do then? It is no good simply wishing them away. Our mindsets are there for good reasons.

Earlier we thought of mindsets as windows through which we view the world outside. But, like any window, we can also look through them the other way, towards the inside. This is what we must do if we wish to change a particular belief or attitude. We must look back through the window into our inner worlds, and explore what is anchoring it.

Behind most of our mindsets is an inner need or motivation. We may believe that money is important because it helps satisfy our need for security. We may assume that by telling others how to behave we will be able to exercise more control over them. Or, if we have a prejudice against another person it may be because he threatens our desire for recognition and approval.

In these examples the need which the mindset fulfils is fairly apparent, but this is not always so. Often it is much more difficult to see. In most cases we are not even aware of our underlying needs, let alone being clear on how they influence our mindsets.

The relationship between needs and mindsets, and the behaviour they generate, is well illustrated by a situation which occurred on a creative management programme we were running for one of our US clients. We came down to breakfast early to prepare for the day ahead. The vice-president of one of the divisions was already sitting at a table on his own. Out of courtesy, we explained that we needed to talk together and excused ourselves from joining him. 'That's OK,' he replied. But as we were walking away, he added, half-jokingly, 'But don't expect me to buy you a drink tonight!' We both felt this was a rather odd and unnecessary remark, but said nothing.

Later that day, as part of the programme, we were looking at the needs and values behind mindsets, and how they affect our behaviour. During this session the same vice-president, somewhat embarrassed, asked how this would explain what he had said at breakfast. It transpired that he had also felt his reaction had been rather immature. Moreover he recognized that this behaviour was a common pattern for him, and one he did not like.

As we explored the mindset that lay behind this particular behaviour, it became clear that he did not fully believe our reason for wanting to sit elsewhere was so that we could plan our day. He was telling himself, 'They want to avoid sitting with me – they are rejecting me.'

What was behind this assumption? He began to realize that he wanted to be recognized and approved of by others, and to feel that he belonged to the group. Beneath these needs was an even stronger need to be loved, not in the romantic sense, but to be accepted and appreciated as a human being. In excusing ourselves from sitting with him, we had unknowingly (both to him and ourselves) posed a threat to these needs, leading him to feel rejected.

He then saw that these needs lay behind not just this particular incident, but many other similar responses. They made him vulnerable, especially when in situations which could be interpreted as rejection. His habitual behaviour in response to this mindset had been to react by attacking back and rejecting others. And he used humour to hide it.

As he began to understand this mechanism he saw that both the mindset and his reactive behaviour were totally inappropriate for an adult, even though as a young adolescent they had served to protect him. What is more, they seldom gave him the love and recognition he desired. More often he created a self-fulfilling prophecy and was indeed rejected.

What was missing was the ability to acknowledge his needs to be recognized, belong and be loved, and to take responsibility for them in his life. Once he began to look back through the mindset to what was behind it, he could relate to these needs more directly, and take steps to modify his behaviour.

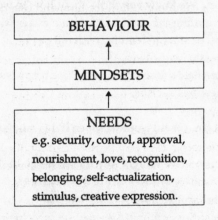

Figure 8.1. This model represents a dynamic interaction. All three levels constantly interact and influence one another. We tend to believe that the outer environment determines our behaviour. While this may be partly true, our behaviour is also determined by our inner environment – our own personal needs.

The dynamic between needs, mindsets and our behaviour illustrated by this case can be summarized in the simple model shown in Figure 8. There is nothing whatsoever wrong with these inner needs. They are always there, and always trying to get satisfied. They are fundamental to our life as human beings, and part of our inner reality.

CHANGING OUR MINDSETS

In the above example the person found it relatively easy to uncover the need that lay behind a particular mindset. But for many of us it can, at first, seem a perplexing task. It is as if we do not know quite what we are looking for. In addition, we have to look for it in the dark. It is rather like the first time we laid hands on a computer. We knew very little about how to work with it. Yet, just as handling the computer became easier with time, so too we can become more familiar with our personal needs and how they operate in our lives.

We can often help this search to get behind a mindset by asking ourselves questions such as,

- What am I afraid would happen if this mindset were not there?
- What do I fear I might lose if I did let go of this belief?
- When and why did I create this mindset?
- What does this mindset help me get?

You personally may find some of these questions more useful than others, and some easier to answer than others. You may also find that there are other questions that are more helpful to you. The purpose behind all the questions is to get at what is anchoring a particular mindset in place. Looking at the answers that come up, you can probably begin to get a feel for the need that is operating. It may help to look back at some of the examples of needs listed in Figure 8.1. Do not be surprised if you find there is more than one need at work.

Simple questions such as these helped a factory supervisor understand and change a disagreeable behaviour in his domestic life. Occasionally his 14-year-old daughter would stay out late drinking with friends. Although he did not object to alcohol in itself, his initial response was to get furious, lose his temper and confiscate her wardrobe and make-up. After a few days he would become contrite and apologize for what then seemed extreme and unjustified behaviour. But try as he would, he had been unable to respond differently when the situation recurred.

Exploring the thinking that lay behind his behaviour, he fairly easily uncovered the mindset. He believed that by taking away her clothes and make-up he would keep her at home, and so prevent her staying out late drinking. To discover what needs this mindset was serving, he tried answering questions similar to those above.

What did he fear he would lose if he let go of this belief? The feeling of being in control of his daughter.

How did this belief help him? Because of his love for his daughter, and his sense of responsibility, he did not want her drinking at this early age. Again he wanted to have some influence over her behaviour.

Once he saw what was motivating his irrational reactions, he realized that there were other ways in which he could satisfy his need to influence her. He sat down with her, treated her more as an adult, talked about his own concerns, and worked out a better solution with her about appropriate boundaries for her at this stage in her life.

In short, it is not our needs themselves that cause us problems, but the mindsets we hold concerning the best way to satisfy them. Ways of meeting a need which may have served us earlier in life can over time become ossified mindsets. Rather than helping us meet our needs, such attitudes often stand in our way. If we can recognize our deeper needs and listen to what they are telling us about ourselves, we can often find better, more appropriate ways to address the need. In effect, we release the anchor holding the mindset in place. The result is a much greater choice in how we think and act.

OTHER PEOPLE'S NEEDS

Having discovered the needs behind some of our own behaviours we tend to assume that others follow the same pattern. But this may not be the case. Compare the needs of the person who drives fast because of a need for excitement and stimulation with those of a person who drives fast because driving wastes time. The behaviour is the same; the needs are very different.

The difficulty in knowing which particular needs underlie a behaviour is a problem faced by any organization trying to motivate its staff. A large software house was having difficulty retaining some of its brightest young programmers. It was spending a great deal of time and money training them, only to have them leave after a year or two and join other houses. The company was paying these people top salaries, providing excellent work environments, and offering fringe benefits beyond the industry norm. But still staff kept leaving.

The mistake that senior management had made was to assume that these people were motivated primarily by material needs. When they took time to investigate what they really wanted, they found a strong need for personal autonomy, creativity and self-expression. But the size and complexity of the projects they

THE INNER WORLD OF THE CREATIVE MANAGER

were working on required teams of ten or more, and there was little opportunity to satisfy these more personal needs. In most of the companies that the young staff were moving to, the projects were smaller and the teams more intimate, allowing a greater expression of individual creativity.

Another example of misunderstood motivations occurred some time ago on a tea plantation in India. The owner decided to increase his workers' motivation by doubling their wages. The result was that they turned up half as often.

OUR COMMON SEARCH

Beneath all these various motivating forces is one motivation that we all share. Whatever we do, we do because we hope that, in one way or another, it will reduce either internal discomfort or make us feel better. Put very simply, our underlying goal is a happier state of mind. This is our most fundamental motivation. It underlies everything we do, and it is a motivation that we all share.

We eat because we know we do not like feeling hungry. We may seek promotion because we believe it will make us happier. We may try to do a job well for the satisfaction it brings us. Some listen to music in order to feel at ease. Others seek solitude because they think it will give them peace of mind. People may help others because it gives them a sense of fulfilment. A few even commit suicide because that seems better than continuing to feel the way they do. Whatever we do, we are seeking to increase our inner well-being.

This even applies to the basic needs discussed above. They too are fuelled by this search. We believe that having security will give us peace of mind; that receiving recognition will bring us happiness; that being in control will give us a sense of freedom;

that a sense of belonging will make us feel better; or that self-actualization will bring fulfilment.

Yet we also know in our hearts that none of these are necessarily the case. We know of people who have all the security they could dream of, and are still not at peace; of individuals who have recognition the world over, but who have not found inner fulfilment; and of those who have control, influence and power beyond measure, yet still are not happy. What we so easily forget is that it is not security, recognition or control we really want, but peace of mind.

Recognizing this in our daily lives is crucial to our achieving the happiness we seek. Here again some simple questions can be of help. Whenever you find yourself attached to the idea that some thing or other is necessary for your inner well-being and happiness, you can try asking yourself,

• If I do not get what I want, can I still have peace of mind? and,

• Even if I do get what I want, will it really bring me peace of mind?

We may believe that only by reaching our sales target will we be able to feel happy at the year-end. But is that really true? We may tell ourselves that if we do not receive the promotion we have sought, we cannot be content. But is this really so? Or we may think that our partner has to behave in a certain way, for us to be happy. But is this true? And even if they did, would fulfilment then be ours?

The important thing is to recognize that we always have a choice. We can choose how we perceive and judge a given situation, and hence choose how we respond to it. If we see things as a threat – a threat to a mindset of what we must have in order to be at peace – then we will not be at peace. On the other hand, while it may not be easy, there is always the possibility of seeing things in other ways, as opportunities rather than threats.

This choice of perception is a choice we have at every moment of the day. The more we learn how to exercise this choice, the more we can become the masters of our thoughts, our feelings and our behaviour. And the more free we will be to respond creatively to the situations in which we find ourselves.

Chapter 9

CREATIVE MANAGEMENT WITH OTHERS

No one is wise enough by himself.
Titus Maccius Plautus (c. 200 BC)

There are children playing in the street who could solve some of my top problems in physics, because they have modes of sensory perception that I lost long ago.
J. Robert Oppenheimer

Creative managers are not just concerned with their inner realities: they are men and women of action. As such they are inevitably in interaction with others, and through this interaction the power and influence of their creative impulses are magnified.

Working with others enables us to go beyond our personal weaknesses and limitations. It allows us to draw upon resources that are beyond the means of any individual, and to move from personal endeavours to large-scale operations. This group effort is the foundation stone of any organization.

Thus, important as it may be for us to develop our own inner resources, it is equally important for us to attend to our relationships with others, and support others in their creative process.

CREATIVE RELATIONSHIPS

Although we are each individuals, we are not creatures of isolation. We are always relating to other people, whether at work, at home, or in our social community. These relationships may range from intimate personal relations to more formal business relations, and from contacts we make every day to those that we make only very occasionally. Yet, important and ubiquitous as our relationships may be, most of us find them one of the most difficult areas of our life. Few would say there is no room for improvement.

Many of us treat our relationships as something 'out there' that we have little influence over. They are good, bad or indifferent, and that is that. Often people say, that is just the way the other person is. They fail to see that the quality of our interaction is our mutual responsibility. In this respect a relationship is something we create. It is something in which the creative process is always present.

Relationships may have times of frustration. One of our colleagues may not behave as we would like; we may not understand a customer; or we may not feel heard ourselves. There are many periods of incubation when we are apart from our associates, and let the connection lie. There are moments of insight when we understand more clearly another's reality, see why he is as he is, and experience a closer connection with him. There is the ongoing process of 'working out' the relationship, resolving misunderstandings, integrating differing needs and exchanging new ideas. In addition, everything that happens between two people can be seen as part of a continuing 'preparation' for future interaction.

When we do pay attention to the quality of our relationships, it is more often than not our more intimate personal connections that we focus on. Yet it is equally important to nurture and care for our professional relationships, for they directly influence the quality of our work. One of the captains of industry interviewed in Francis Kinsman's *The New Agenda* on the future of business said:

> The importance of interpersonal relationships is a peak thing and good managers of people – people people – will be badly needed throughout business. The revolution in communication means that there will be a block between the older generation managers and a new generation with these new skills . . . This is not only a matter of pure communication but actually something closer to consultation and togetherness – the feeling of oneness.

This view was echoed by another corporate leader, Robert Staubli, president of Swissair, at a European symposium on long-term questions of the future:

> There are sound reasons for emphasizing – some might say over-emphasizing – work on the capability of community. In a company, the estimated loss of potential in performance ranges from 30 to 50%, due to interhuman problems, unsettled conflicts, inhibitions, troubled relations, insufficient freedom, and a lack of opportunities for development. I think this estimate is cautious.

Working at our relationships is not easy, however. Like many other of the less material and less tangible aspects of our lives, we are taught very little (if anything) at school or college about this art. Most of us grow up with little awareness of the care and attention that they require. Then later, as we come to realize the importance of working on them, we probably find we do not have the necessary understanding and interpersonal skills. We do not know how to take responsibility for them. Sometimes we believe the other person should take more care. At other times we live in hope that they will work out well, more or less of their own accord. But this seldom works.

COMMUNICATION

The essence of any relationship is communication. It is communication, in one form or another, that links people together. It is the fabric of human society.

The word 'communication' comes from the Latin *communis*, meaning 'common' or 'shared'. In its original sense, it is the creation of a common understanding, a sharing of experience between people. This can take many different forms. We may share agendas, strategies, objectives, problems, wishes, news and even idle gossip. We may share past experiences, ideas and insights, hopes and fears, feelings and emotions. We may share in words, in body language, in the looks we give each other, in the tone of our voice, and also in what we do not say. We may share through music, art, dance, and all the other expressions of our creativity.

Yet it is surprising how careless we can be over something that is so important to our lives and work. We are usually very careful with something that is physically shared – like property, a company, or money – yet show far less care when it comes to sharing our thoughts and emotions. Too often a communication does not result in a shared experience. It is often more like the statement, 'I know you believe you understand what you think

I said, but I am not sure you realize that what you heard is not what I meant.'

Communication, being a flow of information between people, involves us as both senders and receivers. Improving the quality of our communication therefore requires that we attend both to what we send and how we send it, and to how well we receive what others give us.

SHARING OUR FEELINGS

Much of what we share in our interactions is at the level of ideas and experience. We tell of what has happened to us, share our learnings, explain our thinking, ask questions, give answers, show our intentions, supply information, direct others, convey our wishes, etc. But this is not all there is to communication. It becomes richer and far more valuable if we can create an atmosphere of openness, trust and mutual respect so that we can also share our more personal thoughts and intimations, our feelings and emotions, our hopes and fears, our vulnerabilities and misgivings, our deeper wishes and aspirations, our feelings of anger and frustration, our sensitivities and intuitions, our excitements and joys, our ideals and truths. True communication involves the sharing of any and all of life's experiences – and in both verbal and non-verbal ways.

Increasingly, people are appreciating the need for deeper, more personal forms of communication. Yet many are also discovering that this is not easy. If our interaction has hitherto been largely in terms of facts and figures, goals, strategies, performance and agreements, we may find it very hard to start talking of our feelings.

Underlying this difficulty is the fact that most of us do not even have the right vocabulary. It is surprising how often a manager, when asked how he 'feels' about something, replies, 'I think . . . ' followed by some judgement or assessment as to its value or worth: 'I think it is useful for us,' or, 'I think it shouldn't be allowed.' It can often take some time before he realizes that these are not feelings, but thoughts. When the difference does dawn, it may still take some inner exploration before he can find the right words: 'I feel frustrated that this meeting hasn't achieved what I expected,' 'I feel resentful that . . .,' 'I feel expectant,' 'I feel uncertain,' or 'I feel joyous.'

Learning to express our emotions can take a lot of practice. Even when we have the vocabulary, and know what it is we are feeling inside, it is not always easy to share it with others. We may fear embarrassment, looking foolish or appearing soft, or we may be afraid of the other's reactions. Yet it can be a most valuable step in almost any area of business. In the case of the chemical company mentioned in Chapter 2, it was only after people had expressed their emotions that resolution became possible. Although at the level of ideas, there was polarization, the feelings they had were common. But they had to share them before they could see it.

COMMUNICATING THE TRUTH

Perhaps the most important lesson in communication, and the lesson many of us have to learn over and over again, is always to tell what is true – although this does not mean having to tell everything. Not being open and honest about our feelings may seem to get us through short-term difficulties in a relationship, but it does not help in the long-term. If we do not communicate what is true for us, then we can hardly expect the quality of our relationship to remain high.

This was put very clearly by the vice-president of personnel in an American retail outfit:

So many of these guys hide their tensions. We haven't woken up to the fact that hiding them is more of a threat than exposing them. Getting them to talk about why they feel uptight in the same way that they talk about the budget figures, the margins, the marketing strategies, and the training that they just attended, is the hardest thing. The problem is being prepared to take the risk and expose the soft underbelly. It all comes down to being honest with each other.

Being truthful does not mean that we always say things which we know others will find hurtful, or share everything that is going on inside us. But it does mean not saying things which are untrue. If, on being asked how we are, we reply, 'OK,' when we know inside that we are not, we are not telling the truth. We are just taking an easy way out – and, more often than not, the other person knows it. It would be more honest to say 'No, I'm not OK, but I do not feel I can (or want to) talk about it at the moment.'

Nor does telling the truth mean that we have to blurt it out directly – and often clumsily. We should take care over the process. If, for example, we want to tell somebody an uncomfortable truth, we can often make it far easier for ourselves (and for the other person) if we first share what is true about how we are feeling. We might say, 'Look, there is something I need to talk about, but I'm finding it very difficult to get started and I'm afraid of how you might react. I'm also not sure that I can express myself clearly, and I'm concerned that you may not understand me properly.' This is just as honest as blurting out the other more uncomfortable facts. But by first sharing our emotional truths we open up the way we relate. It is usually then easier to talk about the more difficult issues.

PUTTING TRUTH ON THE TABLE

Communicating these hidden deeper truths is essential to our effective working together in groups. Employees are increasingly demanding full and truthful communication – from their boss, from their colleagues, and also from themselves. While they want a warm and friendly environment, they also want one in which honesty is valued. They want to see difficult issues on the table, not pushed under the carpet, hidden and unspoken, or glossed over with half-truths. Summarizing his survey of senior management, Francis Kinsman writes:

> Managers will have to be more communicative to the workers, exposing their own vulnerability and their mistakes and making themselves responsive to the employees' minds. A subsequent growth of mutual respect will mean that things are easier to do in the long run. But before they do it will be necessary for managers to show their humanity first. Can management dare to show its personal problems and be open with the workforce? And if it does will the workforce dare to listen? The answer is yes, yes, yes.

Colin Marshall, chief executive of British Airways, speaking at the Institute of Directors in London, put it even more succinctly: 'Always tell the truth – it usually is rather effective.' It may not always be easy, but as the inventor/architect/philosopher Buckminster Fuller observed, 'If everyone spoke the truth, and only the truth, all of the time, there would be no problems in the world.'

Disclosing our unspoken thoughts can have other advantages. One of us recently got together for an afternoon with two colleagues to discuss possible ways of continuing our work together. Just as we were about to finish, one of them said, 'This idea keeps coming into my mind. It sounds silly, and it probably won't work for you two, but how about we go away together for a few days to explore some of the things that are really exciting to us; then invite some of our corporate friends to join us for the second half, and run a spontaneous programme which is right on our cutting edge?' The other two of us instantly approved of the idea. By honouring her inner voice, and expressing it, however silly it may have seemed, she had come up with the most exciting idea of the afternoon.

Echoes of a 'one-liner' from our friend Ray Gottlieb immediately came to mind: 'Declare your hidden agenda; it may be the best idea around.'

LISTENING

Inept as most of us may be at expressing our inner worlds, we are even poorer at receiving what others have to say. Sometimes we do not even hear the words another is saying, let alone understand the real intention behind them. More often we are more interested in the messages we are sending out than we are in receiving the messages sent to us. Yet good listening is essential to any communication – and to any relationship.

As with poor expression, the costs of poor listening are high. Michael Ray and Rochelle Myers point out in their book, *Creativity in Business*, that:

> For the lack of listening, billions of dollars of losses accumulate : retyped letters, rescheduled appointments, rerouted shipments, breakdowns in labor management relations, misunderstood sales presentations, and job interviews that never really got off the ground.

Moreover it is not just listening to the words that is important; we must also learn to understand what is behind the words. There was the senior manager in the National Health Service, mentioned earlier, who felt that his colleagues had never really understood his difficulties. We have come across instances of marketing managers who had a feeling that the latest product line would not sell well, but, because they could not express their hunches easily, went unheard until it was too late. There are many cases of people saying they are OK, but really meaning the opposite.

Take, for example, the managing director of a British manufacturing company who had, for a long time, been concerned about one of his general managers. But the general manager repeatedly said that everything was fine and he was coping well. The managing director had taken his words at face value, but had failed to hear the underlying message. When he did so he was very troubled by what he found:

> Now, for the first time, I'm beginning to understand how he feels, and I'm realizing how stressed he is. He has always been so positive and committed to the company and would carry out all the directives he was given. But the communication has all been one-way, from us to him. There's been no listening to him. Now we've got to act fast, otherwise it is clear he could become a very sick man.

We know that communication is a two-way process, involving both sender and receiver, yet we often behave as if good communication was only a question of being an expert and polished sender. Part of the reason is that listening skills are something that few of us are taught. It is far easier to teach the skills of clear expression, for these, being things that you can *do*, are tangible skills. But good listening is not something you do as an activity, it is more an attitude of mind and an exercise of the attention. It is an inner process, and therefore much harder to handle.

In this respect listening bears close parallels to the inner phases of the creative process. Preparation and implementation are things we can *do*, and our training has given us various skills and techniques to manage these phases. Managing the frustration, incubation and insight stages is, however, much more difficult. They are more mysterious, far less tangible, and much harder to 'teach'.

We work with these more inner phases not by 'doing' so much as stepping back and trying to hear inwardly what it is we are trying to tell ourselves. We are listening to our own inner voice. It is not therefore surprising to find that the qualities of mind so important for these aspects of creativity – receptivity, relaxation and an open mind – are also a key to listening well to others.

LISTENING AND SELF-TALK

As with creativity, our mindsets often get in the way of our listening. They appear as the 'self-talk' that goes on inside our heads. This is not the quiet inner voice that we discussed in the previous chapter. It is a much louder, far more conscious voice, that interrupts our thinking. It is the voice that wants to add to what is being said; that says, 'Yes ... but ... ' and starts composing our own response; that wonders, 'What's his hidden agenda?' 'Did he understand what I said?' 'Is she getting at me?' 'Should I close the deal now?' 'When will they finish?' It is the voice that wishes we had not started this conversation; that says, 'I bet he's been talking to my boss'; that suddenly remembers we must call somebody.

At times this self-talk may be useful, but it can also interfere with our listening. We can only focus on one thing at a time. So long as our attention is taken up by the voice in our head, we are not fully listening to the voice of the other person.

The level of self-talk can often be reduced simply by becoming aware of it. Noticing that we have gone off on an inner tangent can be enough for us to wake up and return our attention fully to the other person – assuming, that is, that our intention is to listen. If we are being truly honest in our listening, we might even interrupt the speaker to say, 'I'm sorry, I wandered off for a moment. Could you please repeat that last bit just so I can be sure I got it.' Although most of us would find such an admission an embarrassment, and prefer to be less active in our listening, few speakers find it offensive. More often they appreciate our willingness to hear and understand.

In the longer term our self-talk can be another window on ourselves. Much of it comes from some inner fear. We may be afraid that we may not have the chance to express ourselves, that we are not in control, that the other may not approve of us, or that we will not get what we want. Most of the time these fears are irrational; they only arise because some mindset or need is threatened. Noticing the kind of self-talk that repeatedly comes up for us in conversation allows us to step back and become more aware of these deeper issues, and be less at their mercy. Thus, somewhat paradoxically, although our self-talk may block our listening, truly hearing what it is telling us can free us to listen more fully to others.

GIVING FEEDBACK

When listening, we should remember that we cannot know whether or not we have understood without getting feedback.

Another may ask, 'Have you understood?' and we may reply, 'Yes,' believing that we have, but how do we know? Have we 'heard what they really meant'? The only way to find out is to check.

Before we respond to what the other person has said, we might say, 'Let me just check I've got it right. What I heard you saying is . . . ' and then briefly summarize what he has said in our own words. Again, this is something that many of us find difficult – mainly because it is not something that people usually do. But it invariably leads to clearer communication, and often nips misunderstandings in the bud.

Giving feedback frequently seems totally unnecessary. When asked to do this as an exercise, a manager we know was very reluctant to engage in feedback to his boss. 'I know what he's saying,' he said. 'It's simple to understand, and he's said it to me before.'

Yet when he did eventually feed back what he thought had been said, he was surprised to hear his boss reply, 'No, you haven't heard the most important bit.' In this case it took several exchanges before the manager was able to summarize the message to the other's satisfaction. Had he not done so, the hidden misunderstanding would undoubtedly have continued to dog their relationship for a few more years.

In addition to ensuring that a communication is clearly received, engaging in feedback also improves our listening skills. Having the intention of summarizing the other person's point of view can be a major help in focusing our attention on what the other person is saying. Our intention to hear will be much greater, and the voice in our head that much quieter.

In making this effort to listen more deeply, we are in effect saying, 'I want to hear you,' 'I want to understand you better,' 'I want to appreciate what is true for you.' Not only does this enhance communication, it can also have a dramatic effect on the quality of the way we relate. As we begin to hear other people more fully, and are in turn heard better by them, we often discover not only the differences between us, but also the range of common ground we share.

VALUING DIFFERENCE

At a deep level we are all very similar. We are each seeking to improve our feeling of inner well-being. We all have values that in one way or another we want to express. We all have needs we are trying to fulfil, although the nature of the need may vary from one person to another. We all have mindsets – some that help us, and some that get in our way. We each experience pressure, but respond in different ways; some may see a demand as a welcome challenge, others may see it as a major threat. Similarly, the process of creativity is fundamentally the same for each of us; yet we each have areas where we are strong and confident, and others where we are weaker.

Valuing differences is a key to successful management, as Ralph Kilmann brings out so clearly in his book *Beyond the Quick Fix*:

> The most enlightened managers today are those who take pride in reaching out for help from whomever they can get it. These managers know their limitations and accept them as part of their human makeup. They are the first to recognize what they can do effectively by themselves and when they need to enlist the aid of others. It is not a matter of massaging egos – it is a matter of doing what is necessary to solve complex problems. The enlightened manager looks for diversity of inputs as a natural and recurring part of his job.

As the problems we are required to tackle continue to become more and more complex and inter-related, teamwork becomes more and more of a necessity. Letting go of our mindsets about independence can be difficult, however. The new head of a growing seafood company had been struggling to find ways of bringing his organization into line with the needs of the 1990s. The old-style managing director of a seafood company had to be 'all things to all people'. He was the buyer, production manager and salesman. Today, the rapidly changing marketplace and the increasing pressures the industry is under meant that he needed to build a team with specialist skills.

> We have a much more complex set of problems than we did 15 years ago. EEC fishing regulations, Japanese fish farming, the dumping of stocks, the increasing sophistication and discrimination of the consumer and new marketing practices, mean that I can no longer plan the business on my own. I must now draw on the skills of our senior management team.
>
> None of us can do it alone. We can't even come near, even though we sometimes think we can. We not only have to work together, we depend on one another. Our skills are different and we each bring something different to the party and that's what makes it possible. We need the humility and courage to recognize our limitations and make it work for the company as a whole, otherwise we won't survive for long.

The recognition of the need for teamwork pervades all organizations and all levels of management, from the top to the factory floor. Team-building figures high on most internal agendas, various experiments have been tried, and important insights and practice have been gained in understanding how teams work.

Different theories and models have been developed, and there are now a variety of methods of exploring individual roles and team profiles. Yet, despite this continuing investment of time and energy, getting a team to gel is for many still a mysterious process.

While much of the work on team-building has gone a long way in understanding the complex social and interpersonal issues at play, there are deeper personal issues that need to be addressed. These are seldom voiced and difficult to observe. Even when they are, they may not fit easily into the models.

We often regard these more elusive and puzzling human traits as unnecessary weaknesses and personal foibles. We expect people to act without hidden agendas or personal needs – that is, to be the perfectly rational team member. Unfortunately, such perfect team members do not exist.

This is not to imply that current models are wrong, only that they are partial. It is equally important to learn to manage the more unpredictable human processes which are to be found in every team.

THE HUMAN FACE IN A TEAM

Attending to these more mystifying dimensions can, as we have seen, be a much more challenging task than managing the more familiar and tangible aspects. This was brought out very clearly with a client's senior management group. Over a period of twelve years, the president of the corporation had built up a team of able and experienced people, each committed to the company. They knew each other well, recognized each other's strengths and weaknesses, and realized that working together as a strong team was important. But in recent years something seemed to be missing.

The president's solution was to take them away for a few days to the mountains. There they could all have a good time together, away from the demands of the office, and come to know each other a little better. At the same time they could get agreement on next year's corporate goals and longer-term strategies, and so create a renewed sense of team spirit. With us there to run an exciting programme and fire them with enthusiasm, the president believed he had a good formula for success.

Around lunchtime on the first day, however, it became clear that much more would be needed. Body language, tone of voice, odd remarks by some and silence on the part of others suggested that there was a lot that was not being said. With some gentle encouragement the hidden feelings slowly began to come out – and their appearance surprised many of the group, particularly the president.

They clearly knew each other well in terms of their experience, expertise, abilities, likes and dislikes, and how each would be likely to behave in a particular situation, or respond to a specific challenge. But there their acquaintance stopped. They did not really know each other in terms of what was important to them and why they behaved in the way they did.

One of the more surprising things that emerged concerned the financial director's attitude towards the president over an issue that had happened ten years previously. The group all knew of the past disagreement, and everyone thought that, since the issue itself had been resolved and never spoken of again, the rift had been healed and forgotten. On the surface it had, but not in the financial director's mind. Although it was no longer a big issue for him, he still felt that he had been misunderstood and wronged all those years ago, and feared a repetition. His fear was not something that he lost any sleep over, and he saw that it was probably irrational and unjustified given the current circumstances; but still it was there in the back of his mind, preventing him from feeling completely at ease with the group.

It is unexpressed fears such as these that are the incipient poison in any relationship. It always seems easier to keep quiet and avoid either looking foolish or upsetting someone else. Yet the very fact that they are withheld creates a separation between the people concerned. Part of our role was to create a safe environment in which the financial director would not feel judged, and the others would be open to hearing him. With some difficulty he began to talk about his concern with the rest of the group. As he did, he found that it was not the fear of a similar event recurring that was standing in his way, but the fear of appearing irrational to the rest of the team.

The group was somewhat surprised to hear that he still, after all these years, held a mild resentment towards the president – particularly the president himself, who thought that all had been forgotten. Their reaction, however, was not one of criticism or rejection, but of relief. Now they could understand why he sometimes behaved the way he did in meetings. It was not just a personality quirk; there was a reason behind it.

The outcome was that, by sharing more of his inner world, he included himself more in the group. And the more that his colleagues understood him, the more they were able to open up to him. A more significant result, however, was a major transformation in his relationship with the president. They were able to heal the past in a way that had not been possible so long as part of the past had been kept hidden.

Once the financial director had shared his own concerns, others in the group were able to talk more freely about themselves. One was able to talk for the first time of his need for security, and how that affected so much of his life, including his work in the company. Another who had always been the quiet member of the group, and whom the president had taken to be a rather less strong team member, began to speak of his shyness, and then of his vision for the company, revealing a commitment to his work far deeper than anyone had suspected.

The group did not end up having the exciting 'gung-ho' time they had expected. Instead, they began to see that what was really missing from their team was true communication. It became a time of group discovery, the development of a deeper mutual understanding and personal caring, providing the foundation for a far more solid team.

MANAGING THE TEAM PROCESS

Managing a team is not always as easy as it was in the above case. More often it is an ongoing process, with its own frustrations, learnings and breakthroughs. Rather than taking teams away to the country to fire them with enthusiasm or for heart-to-heart meetings, what is often required is a sustained awareness of the human concerns present in any group of people, and the ability to handle the team process.

Within these more subtle and personal team dynamics we again find elements of the creative process at work. People do not usually come together as a team immediately; they generally need an initial period of 'preparation' and settling in. There are periods of frustration and discomfort as people begin to find their place together, or hit unresolved issues. There are times when individuals may need to work on their own, and times when the whole team will need to take a break and 'incubate'. For facilitating insights and breakthroughs a receptive environment is important. And finally, there are times of intense activity when some, or all, of the group are actively involved in 'working out'.

As with the creative process, there is much that can be done to facilitate the inner aspects of the team process:

• Set aside time at the beginning of a meeting for people to talk briefly about how they are, what they are feeling, and, when appropriate, their hopes and fears, and any issues they may be struggling with. Do not force this, but concentrate more on creating an environment where this is possible.

• Do not rush straight into the agenda. Recognize that any group, however well acquainted they may be, always need some time to 'come together'. People need time to settle and feel at ease; they need to feel heard and accepted as part of the group. The less often they meet and the less well they know each other, the longer this process will take.

• Get the hidden human agendas on the table. Although this may seem to take up valuable time, it is an investment that repeatedly pays off. You are creating a climate within which the team will work far more smoothly and tackle more effectively the official issues on the table. You may feel that this is opening a can of worms; but if there *is* a can of worms, the sooner it is opened and the worms released the better – they can do far more harm hidden in the can.

• Remember that the best way to encourage others to talk about personal issues is to en-courage yourself, and talk about any concerns and feelings you may have. Put your own hidden agenda on the table.

• Above all, handle other people's personal feelings and concerns with the sensitivity, care and compassion with which you would like your own to be handled.

Because it is unfamiliar to most of us managing the inner process of a team is difficult, and often seems like working in the dark. But, if we are to find the key to getting teams to work together well, we have to look in the darkness as well as where there is light. This is why the creative manager is not just a charismatic leader – although he may sometimes take on that role. More importantly, he is also managing the people and the process of the team, thereby enabling the individuals in the team to manage their own inner worlds.

CREATIVE TEAMS

Because the creative process takes place within us, we tend to think it is something we do on our own. Yet the process requires of us a range of skills and abilities – from analytic and rational thinking, to imaginative and visionary skills; from the capacity to step back and see things calmly in perspective, to the dynamic, pragmatic skills of the implementer; from the ability to discover and challenge our assumptions, to the willingness to listen to our inner knowing.

Few of us excel in all these areas. Some of us are good at seeing the essence of a problem; some at stepping back and seeing where we have become stuck; some at coming up with new ideas; and others at testing or implementing proposals. Clearly, if we are to draw upon our creative potential to the maximum and express it fully in our work, we need also to draw upon the strengths of others.

The ways in which a group can pool its individual creative

skills has been explored in considerable depth by Meredith Belbin at the Henley Management College in England. He was concerned with forming teams that would be good at creative problem-solving. His initial thinking was to put together people who scored high on conventional 'creativity' tests. Yet these teams, full as they were of 'creative' people, were disastrous at solving problems together.

The reasons for this failure are clear once creativity is recognized as a process involving several different phases. Most creativity tests implicitly assume that creativity is about coming up with new ideas. Thus they usually identify 'original thinkers', who are good at the insight phase. Such people tend to be individualists; when several of them are put together in a team, they are all ideas, but no action. No one listens; they are all too busy putting forward their own solutions. There is no one to focus the group; no one to evaluate which ideas are worthwhile; and no one to carry them into practice.

Clearly a truly creative team needs to be able to handle all the phases of the creative process. Besides the idea generators, there need to be good leaders, good researchers, good implementors and good team-builders. Over fifteen years of research with hundreds of teams in a diversity of industries, Belbin has found eight different roles which individuals can play:

> THE PLANT – THE ORIGINAL THINKER. This is the person who scores high on most creativity tests, the 'ideas-generator'. Belbin calls him 'a plant' because in his early research such people were 'planted' into teams to see if they would enhance team creativity. They often seem withdrawn and quiet; but they are usually thinking, and will suddenly come out with very original ideas.

THE RESOURCE INVESTIGATOR. This person also brings new ideas into a group, but the ideas come from his interaction with others, rather than 'out of the blue'. Much more sociable than the plant, he tends to be out and about, talking to people, seeing what others have done, reading, picking up new ideas from others and developing them.

THE CHAIRMAN. He (or she) co-ordinates the efforts of the team to meet external goals and targets. He sees others' strengths and weaknesses and makes sure that all voices are heard; he keeps the process of the team in balance. He welcomes contributions, listens well, sums up, and, if a decision is to be made, makes it firmly on behalf of the group. But the chairman may not necessarily be the team leader.

THE SHAPER. This is another leadership role, complementing that of the chairman, often a dominating, extrovert, 'follow-me' leader. Always keen to get into action, he wants to pull others along with him. Self-confident and results-orientated, he gives 'shape' to the way the team's effort is applied.

THE MONITOR-EVALUATOR. A critic rather than a creator, his contribution is measured and dispassionate analysis of proposals. Sometimes resented by plants and shapers for his 'Yes . . . but . . .' approach, the monitor-evaluator is the one most likely to stop the team from committing itself to a misguided project.

THE ORGANIZER. Also called 'the company-worker'. Disciplined in approach, he turns concepts and plans into practical working procedures. Give him a decision and he will work out a schedule; give him an objective and he will produce an organization chart. He works for the good of the company rather than the pursuit of self-interest.

THE TEAM WORKER. Sensitive to other people, he is aware of individuals' needs and concerns, and perceives most clearly the emotional undercurrents of the group. A good listener and communicator, he encourages others to do the same. He is the facilitator of the team process.

THE COMPLETER-FINISHER. This is the person who guarantees delivery. After a decision is made he likes to be sure that all the details have been checked, and that everyone knows their responsibilities. He is fastidious, conscientious and thorough, making sure that deadlines are met, preserving a sense of urgency in the group.

As you look at these descriptions you can probably see yourself in several of them. It is not that one of us is a 'chairman' and another a 'team worker'; we each possess most of these characteristics to some extent. What is important is to become aware that different roles exist, and see which roles tend to be strongest for us, and which are weaker.

In addition, the roles we play will be different in different groups. A person may appear as a strong shaper in one team, but be much less so in another team where an even stronger shaper is present. Such an analysis is valuable in understanding the role a person takes in a particular team, rather than categorizing a person in a fixed way.

Belbin makes it very clear that there is no formula for designing the perfect team. Successful teams can vary in size from two to ten or more; and many different combinations of team roles are possible. Where his work is most useful is in helping us understand why a particular team may not be performing very creatively – as in the case of a group of 'plants', a team without any plants or resource-investigators, or a team with too many shapers each pulling against each other. It can also be very valuable when putting a team together, in ensuring that all aspects of the creative process are adequately covered.

This sort of evaluation was crucial to a project group in a medium-sized industrial company. On completing the self-assessments that Belbin has developed (see bibliography) they found that the team was very strong in plant and resource-investigator, had good chairman, team worker and completer-finisher qualities. But no one was performing the role of monitor-evaluator. Without such qualities the team was very likely to set off on paths which had not been properly tested and assessed, only to find out months later, and at great cost, that they had acted precipitously.

Seeing this lack, the project leader enlisted the help of a good monitor-evaluator from another division to sit in on their monthly meetings. His task was to listen to their suggestions, bringing to their attention any factors which they might have overlooked, and pointing out areas where he felt they were being unrealistic.

Attending to how people work together as a team is an important step in allowing our creative impulse to flow more effectively into the world; but our work with others does not end there. If we are to be as effective in our work as we would wish, we need not just the support of others; we need their fullest creativity.

EMPOWERMENT

Everyone of us is part of a larger organization – whether it be our family, our project team, our social community, our company or even our species. The changing times we live in, and the new challenges ahead, will require that these and other organizations are able to respond with as much creativity as possible. This means releasing the creativity of as many as possible of the individuals within them. If we are to see our visions and values become more manifest in the world, in our work and in our families, it is not enough to become more creative managers ourselves; we must also seek to help others become the same.

Facilitating another person's development is intrinsic to the management of people. To manage is to 'optimize the use of the resources available'. In people terms, this translates as seeing that individuals use their own potential to the full. In other words, an essential ingredient in any people management, whether at work, at home or socially, is to foster their own creative processes – that is, to help them understand their own inner worlds, trust themselves and their insights, communicate what they truly feel, see their own mindsets and step back from them, be aware of their own hidden motivations, and, perhaps most important if we are all to pull together, be in touch with their hearts and their sense of what truly matters.

Before we jump into trying to help others release their own creativity, however, we should remember just how difficult it is to do this for ourselves. We cannot tell ourselves to be more creative; it is not something we can make happen. This book has tried to show that we must learn to let it happen.

This does not mean that there is nothing we can do to facilitate our own creativity; there are many ways in which we can open up the flow of this innate and most human of impulses – as this book has also tried to show. Becoming more creative is something that grows upon us as we become more aware of our selves and our inner processes – something which Abraham Maslow saw thirty years ago, when he wrote that creativity and self-actualization are very closely linked, and may even turn out to be the same thing.

The same is true when we turn our attention to releasing the creative potential of others. It is no good telling them to be more creative – we cannot *make* others creative – nor can we make them *let it happen*. But there is a lot we can do to help them take this power for themselves.

Take, for example, the creative process itself. It is relatively easy to help others in the more outer phases of preparation and implementation. We can show how we do it, teach skills and give feedback on performance. But when it comes to handling the more inner phases we need to take a somewhat different approach.

Another person's frustration is part of his own process, and not something he should be admonished for. Rather than advising him to snap out of it and get on with the task, we should accept the validity of the experience for him, remembering how we can get caught ourselves.

However, we should also be aware of the temptation of projecting our own experience of frustration on to him, suggesting, for example, that he takes time off to incubate. He may need something very different. What we can do is give him the space to be with how he is feeling at a particular time, and see what his own inner voice may be telling him.

In similar ways we can encourage others to take their own

time for incubation and insight – not chastising subordinates for 'wasting time', for example, when stepping back from the problem for a while may be just what they need; not judging or rejecting another's insight because we cannot immediately see its value, but giving it the same chance to grow that we would give our own.

Once again, it is not so much a different way of 'doing' that is required of us, but a different attitude, a different way of 'being' with others – a way that lets others feel empowered rather than judged or threatened.

THE EMPOWERING PROCESS

Empowerment is one of those oft-used but much misunderstood terms. Empowerment is not something we can do to others – much as though some would like to – it is something that we create for ourselves. It is a sense of freedom we feel inside; a freedom to be who we really are, to draw upon our own resources, and express our own truths. When we feel empowered, we feel alive, alert, in touch with our feelings, responsible, our own authority, valued and free to choose.

But no one 'empowered' us. No one makes us feel that self-worth, just as no one ever *makes* us upset – even though both may sometimes feel that way. Feelings of empowerment are feelings that come from within, from our own selves. Similarly, if we want those we work and live with to feel more empowered in their own lives, we cannot do it to them. What we can do is create an environment in which they can empower themselves.

The following are some things we have found helpful in facilitating this environment; you may well have others you would like to add:

• Honour the dignity and integrity of every person. Beware of judging others just because they think, perceive or behave in ways which are different from your own. Allow them the freedom to be their own unique self. This does not mean that you have to accept their views or actions as correct; exercise discrimination fully. But do not judge their worth as a human being. No one has that right.

• Encourage others to express their feelings and communicate their own truths. And listen to what they have to express – remember we all need to be heard.

• Take time to talk to people. Do so in your own way and a way that they will understand. Trust your own inner voice about how to be with people rather than your mindsets, or how convention dictates.

• Recognize that others have their needs too. Appreciate that their resistance to change may be as deeply personal as yours. Put yourself in their shoes. Try to experience how they might be seeing things, what their beliefs and assumptions might be.

• Trust yourself and be yourself. Your own self-honesty can liberate the same in another. If you don't know the answer, don't pretend you do. Ask colleagues, subordinates and bosses for their input. Value their views and contributions, and so will they.

• Don't lead others to believe they 'should' do something. Disempowering self-talk, such as 'I should', 'ought to' and 'have to', can inhibit our inner freedom.

• Don't make the old way bad. What you or others did before is not wrong, just not appropriate now.

• Remember, beneath everything, we all want much the same.

Working on empowerment is not always easy – especially when people expect that a good manager should tell them what to do. A good example of this was brought out in a meeting we had with a senior manager and members of his team. When questioned on how he saw his role, he replied:

I am the lubricant. That's my role as general manager. My priority is the effective development of human communication, the proper understanding of our objectives, and how we can develop people to achieve their potential within the division. In doing this, we'll realize our business goals, and we will have fun together doing it.

Some of the people in his team did not think this was a sufficient answer, and kept pushing him to be more specific. Interestingly, he remained unmoved. He kept referring them to this notion that he was the 'lubricant' of the group. These were not idle words, this was the way he worked. He made sure that people understood what was to be done, and supported them to do it.

Nor need empowerment be limited to the workplace. Some of our own consulting team have been working intensely with unemployed people out of work in inner-city areas. There is the mother of three who after years of feeling disempowered by external authorities such as the church, teachers and doctors, realized:

> It is not us and them. We are all us. I allow myself to be disempowered. Once I realized this I could accept my own responsibility in managing my life. If I sat back nothing would happen. If I did something, anything could happen. If people did things I didn't like or understand, rather than moan I now ask why? I demand to be involved. My life is too precious to let someone else take responsibility for it.

Another single parent in the same community, after many years in mental hospitals, refused to live a life dependent on drugs or doctors. She drew on her own resources, determined to take responsibility for her own life. She now runs a voluntary project for people suffering in similar ways as she did. By helping and managing herself, she not only empowered herself, she also found a way to help others to do the same.

There are numerous similar examples – the 14-year-old, written off by teachers, who saw life as a challenge rather than a threat and recently came top of his college class in stage management; the community in Belfast who, in the midst of anger and violence, are creating an education centre in a near-derelict house; the prisoner serving life who became a world-renowned sculptor and writer. These are all people who, against the odds, have made it or are making it. They are people who have drawn on their inner resources to manage their own lives. They are people working together, reaching not for the stars, but to live and manage their lives in creative ways.

LEADERSHIP

The leaders of tomorrow will be those who can create environments in which people feel empowered. This is the essence of good leadership. John Harvey-Jones, ex-chairman of ICI, writes in his book *Making It Happen: Reflections on Leadership*,

> Business leadership is itself an honourable, testing, imaginative and creative job. It is not just about the creation of wealth, it is about the creation of a better world for tomorrow and the building and growing of people.

He believes that today's generation of independent-minded individuals will only stay with a company which treats them with the highest degree of self-respect. This means that leaders themselves must also be truthful to themselves. He continues, 'The most difficult task of the manager is ruthless intellectual honesty about his own skills, weaknesses and motives.' Ruthless for him does not mean climbing over colleagues and competitors in the desperate search for material advantage. It is primarily self-criticism.

Similar sentiments were recently expressed by Colin Marshall of British Airways:

> Emperors rule; leaders motivate . . . [they] hold their job by what they inspire their associates to do, not by the diktats they issue . . .
>
> Our scarcest natural resource is leadership. Not the leadership which adorns itself in fuss and feathers, but that which can get people to do things they did not know they could do. Leadership which depends not

on panoply and pageantry, but on an understanding
of, and caring about, the concerns of people.

Another leader who puts the issue of individual growth high
on his agenda is the president of a New York high-tech corporation with whom we have worked:

> I want us to create a climate where at the end of a
> person's career with us they will feel moved to say: 'I
> have used my life with the company in a worthwhile
> way. Not only was it a good company to work for, but
> I grew as a human being – through this experience I
> am a better person in myself.'

RE-VISIONING LEADERSHIP

As well as reconsidering the role of the leader, we also need to
reconsider who the leaders are. The conventional idea of the
leader is the person at the top of hierarchical apex, the one who
sets a tone to the others who follow, the one who 'shows the way'.
But leadership can come in many different forms.

In the team-role model developed by Belbin, the conventional
leader is normally considered to be a person with either 'shaper'
or 'chairman' characteristics. These are certainly roles which
direct the team in their work towards a goal; but the other roles
'lead' in other ways. The 'plant' leads the generation of ideas, the
'team worker' leads the facilitation of the team process, the
'monitor-evaluator' leads the testing of ideas, and the 'completer-finisher' leads ongoing day-to-day work on a project.

The 'leadership' qualities of these and of the other roles are
essential if the team is to function at its maximum. If the person
performing the role of 'monitor-evaluator', for example, is not
able to help the rest of the team feel empowered, then he will not

be able to carry out his own role effectively. Others may not listen to him so well; they may feel threatened by his critiques and withdraw; or they may not trust and value their own qualities and abilities.

As much as we need to rethink our ideas on who is creative and who is a manager, we also need to reframe our notion of leadership. Too easily we see leadership in other people and not the leadership in ourselves, the leadership that we can offer. Yet there is leadership within every person. That leadership comes from an attitude of mind, not necessarily from the qualifications we have or our position. Leaders 'show the way', and this is something we are each capable of.

What the world needs now is not just leaders in the conventional sense, but people who are willing to 'show the way' – people who can empower themselves, take responsibility for their lives and the world they live in, and who can create an environment which allows others to feel empowered. Such leaders do not have to live at the top of the hierarchy; they can come from all levels and from all walks of life. In this sense Gandhi, Mother Teresa, Bob Geldof, Chico Mendes and Christopher Nolan are models of leadership as much as are the presidents of corporations and countries.

There is no 'right' formula for this new type of leader. Some will be charismatic, others will act more quietly. Some may be strong team players, while others may be strong individualists who appear to 'go it alone'. Some will be pushy, others will guide from behind. Some will be emotionally orientated, others more logical and analytic. Some will be introverted and some highly extraverted. Some will lead consciously, others will be surprised by the fact that they are seen as leaders.

What the new leaders must share is not a new outer style so much as a new inner style. They will understand their own motivations as much as what needs to be done. They will bring more of their own inner truth to what they do. They will be people finding the courage to stand for what they value. They will be people who understand that true authority lies in that quiet voice in their hearts. They will be people sharing their own learnings and visions; people encouraging others to become true to their own inner voice, so that together we can guide ourselves through these extraordinary times.

Marilyn Ferguson sums it all up succinctly in her book *The Aquarian Conspiracy*:

> Plato once said that the human race would have no rest from its evils until philosophers became kings or kings became philosophers. Perhaps there is another option, as increasing numbers of people are assuming leadership of their own lives. They become their own central power. As the Scandinavian proverb says, 'In each of us there is a king. Speak to him and he will come forth.'

None of the ideas in this book are new. Some of them may seem new when we first come across them, but on deeper reflection we often find that they resonate with our own personal intimations and inner knowing. They are things we already know.

We know the world is changing faster, presenting us all with new and profound challenges. We know that past ways of dealing with problems are no longer adequate, and that our current attitudes seem to lead to insane solutions. We know our values have to change.

We know we could be more creative than we are. We know the process of creativity is mysterious, and that we cannot force it to happen. We know we can get stuck in the way we see things, and how much this limits our behaviour. We know we need to be more open-minded.

We know it can be difficult to cope with the pressures of life, and that we must manage ourselves better. We know that we need to learn more about ourselves. We know that there is a wise voice within each of us – although we do not always trust it. We know that there are deeper needs and values within all of us that we sometimes do not listen to. We know we want peace of mind. We know we need to value others and their differences. And we know we cannot do it alone.

We also know we are not perfect. We easily forget we know these things.

Yet these inner knowings are all common-sense. They are born of our experience of life. From childhood onwards, at home and at work, from the depths of our sufferings to the height of our joys, we are learning about life. And behind all these learnings are common truths. They are our common sense.

Unfortunately, we often do not believe in ourselves enough to trust our common sense. The conventional 'wisdom' of society conspires against this inner knowing. It leads us into a world of 'make-believe'. We doubt our selves. We keep secret what we know within.

But the truth is out. There is no secret. It is a wisdom we all share. And like all wisdom it is very simple – tell the truth, take time, listen, honour your feelings, respect others, trust yourself, act with courage and have fun.

It is the wisdom of the child, brought alive so beautifully by these words of Robert Fulghum.

> Most of what I really need to know about how to live, and what to do, and how to be, I learned in kinder-garten. Wisdom was not at the top of the graduate school mountain, but there in the sandbox at nursery school. These are the things I learned: share every-thing; play fair; don't hit people; put things back where you found them; clean up your own mess; don't take things that aren't yours; say you're sorry when you hurt somebody; wash your hands before you eat . . .
>
> Warm cookies and cold milk are good for you; live a balanced life; learn some and think some and draw

and paint and sing and dance and play and work everyday some; take a nap every afternoon; when you go out into the world, watch for traffic; hold hands and stick together; be aware of wonder . . .

Think of what a better world it would be if we all – the whole world – had cookies and milk about 3 o'clock every afternoon and then lay down with our blankets for a nap, or if we had a basic policy in our nation and other nations to always put things back where we found them and cleaned up our own messes. And it is still true, no matter how old you are, when you go out into the world, it is best to hold hands and stick together.

THE CREATIVE STORY
OF THE BOOK

Writing this book has been a personal journey in creativity for both of us. It was also a time of inner learning as we discovered what it took for two people to work closely together on the same project. Since the story that unfolded has fascinated us both, and also many others who have wanted to know how two people write a book together, we decided to tell it here.

The journey began in Nigeria. For some time we had been musing upon the idea of putting the material that we were using in our organizational work into the form of a book. Finding ourselves with a free morning we decided to prepare an outline. After two hours we had a very large sheet of paper filled with a detailed 'mind map' of all our ideas, their structure and organization, and the underlying themes we wanted to convey. What we saw enthused us (literally).

Turning this map into a linear book form seemed a relatively easy task. The only difficulty was that both of us had many other commitments. Our solution was to engage a journalist friend to work with us. This plan certainly got us started. It helped us through our time problem, and helped get many of the ideas down on to paper. But something was missing. The book that was developing did not really capture the vision that had so inspired us in Nigeria.

It slowly dawned on us just how difficult it was to convey our thinking to another. We could easily talk about all the material and its structure, and about the style and approach of the book, but it was much more difficult to transfer the underlying spirit to someone who had not lived through our years of working together. Eventually we agreed that the only way to capture this spirit was to write the whole book ourselves. We decided to do what many other co-authors have done. We each took responsibility for the initial preparation of some of the chapters, passing them on to the other for additions and editing.

But this did not seem to get us much further; in fact the book seemed to be moving even more slowly. We were becoming increasingly frustrated, our enthusiasm was waning, and we both began to wonder whether the book would ever be finished. At the same time, however, we noticed that whenever we sat down to work on the book together our initial inspiration and vision flooded back.

Then the truth hit us. The book was coming not from two individual minds, but from our joint thinking. When we were apart the book had no essence, no real life; when we worked together the inspiration returned and the book flowed out of us. Little wonder then that the friend who had tried ghosting the book had found it so difficult. If neither of us could hold the vision on our own, how could we expect a third party to?

There was only one solution. We had to write together. By coincidence, for the first time in the three years since our Nigeria meeting, we both had spare time at the same time. So, taking leave of absence from our partners, we committed our joint mind to the book and went away to a friend's cottage in the country.

That was when the real process of writing began. In less than three months we wrote the whole book, accomplishing far more than we had so far done in nearly three years. (Although it must also be acknowledged that without this previous preparation, these months would not have gone so well.) It was also during these three intensive months that our greatest learnings took place.

We had gone into isolation in order to be free from any distractions, so that we could be completely absorbed by the book and spend much more time discussing it. But we were still stuck with the mindset that we had to work separately on individual chapters. We imagined ourselves sitting at our computers in separate rooms. Freezing weather and lack of space, however, conspired against us, making us share a large downstairs room for writing. Step by step we were forced closer and closer together until, after a few days, one of us had the insight. 'Since this book is something that seems to be coming out of our joint thinking, what are we doing working on different parts of the book on separate tables? Why don't we try working together at the same computer on the same chapter?'

Since that moment, almost every sentence in this book has been written by both of us, simultaneously. We set one of the Macintoshes up beside the fireplace, expanded the typeface to 18-point, and sat back in armchairs thinking together on to the screen. Word-processing, we began to realize, has, in addition to its many other advantages, brought with it a new dimension to collective writing.

Composing jointly on to the same screen encouraged our one-mindedness. It did not really matter whose fingers happened to be on the keyboard, we were thinking together. Very often, after a period of silently studying a piece we had just written, we would utter the same words simultaneously. At other times one of us would see something that the other would have missed on his own – perhaps spotting an incorrect word, a phrase which did not fully express our intention, something missing, or something in excess. Either of us writing on our own would have missed many of these minor points. The result of this 'collective writing' was a higher quality than either of us would have produced individually.

This is not to imply that all was easy. There were many times when we found ourselves stuck in frustration, not finding the right way to express something, or pushing on with a section that was not quite working. But whenever this did happen, the fact that there were two of us enabled us to move beyond it much more rapidly than is possible on one's own. Working alone we often do not even realize that we are stuck in frustration. Working together, we can spot it in the other, bring it into the open, and recognize it for what it is. Having jointly acknowledged our frustration, we could see whether it was time we took a break and relaxed, went for a walk, went out for a meal, or took a fresh look at what we were trying to write.

Open-mindedness, so essential to creativity, was, we found, much enhanced by this arrangement. On our own there is only one mind working, and that mind too easily becomes fixed. A second mind is a continual source of challenge and inspiration.

Working together we could help each other step back and question any assumptions that we were making. We learnt to voice those nagging questions and concerns, which on their own seem silly or intrusive, but which are in fact the inner voice trying to make itself heard. When one of us raised such questions, we took time to listen, trusting the other's inner voice, rather than seeing it as a challenge to ourselves. Without such mutual trust and respect, the creativity that flowed between us would not have been so rich.

To put it another way, two people can hold a state of creative tension much easier than one – though even this does not express fully the rich interplay we enjoyed as we encouraged each other to follow his inner voice, and allowed ourselves to trust the process that was happening between and within us. Perhaps we will never find an adequate way to put the exhilaration we felt into words.

Writing as a team of two taught us to respect our differences in a new way. We were well acquainted with the respective roles we took when consulting or teaching together. When writing, however, our dominant roles became reversed, leading us to a renewed respect for each other's strengths. The more we learnt about each other, the more we were able to support each other, and the process of the book.

A crucial element to the success of this approach was the fact that we shared the same vision. Although we naturally each brought different ideas, different approaches and expressions, and different insights, we both shared the same goal. There was a unity beneath our differences.

Perhaps the greatest learning of all concerned telling what is true. At times this meant expressing our discomforts and frustrations, and honouring the questions and concerns that voiced themselves. At other times it meant being willing to speak or write only what we felt to be true from our own experience. This was important for both of us. We wanted to create a book that appealed to people's inner knowing as well as to their conscious knowing. To do this we had to be continually willing to listen to and express our own inner knowing.

To encourage this we would, at times, ask, 'What does the book want to say?' or 'What does the book want of us at this moment?' This helped us reconnect with our own truth, rather than either of us trying to force the book to say what our surface minds thought best. Again the lesson was one of trust, of not forcing.

Another continual touchstone which we repeatedly used was to ask, 'Where is Life in this section?' Creativity, we believe, is intrinsic to Life, and for the book to reflect our vision we wanted Life to be present throughout.

Trusting also meant being open to the completely unexpected. Two of the chapters were not anticipated at all. We were working on other material, when suddenly a new context and direction burst in, taking us into some of the most exciting writing in the book.

Synchronicity also had its role. Coincidental chains of events arising from our play together sometimes led us to just the material or examples we needed (often without realizing it) at just the right time. Either of us on his own would probably have pushed on, and not allowed the coincidences to unfold as they did.

None of the above is to imply that we developed a formula to follow. More often than not, if our creativity was not flowing so freely, it was because we had become fixed in some formula of how to work together. Each moment was a fresh moment; each piece of writing a fresh challenge. The key was learning to trust: trust our inner voice, trust our feelings, trust each other and trust our joint-mindedness.

In short, neither of us could have written this book alone. Nor could we have written it together had we not recognized that the book was coming from our collective thinking. Moreover, had we not been willing to trust the creative process, in all its aspects, we certainly could not have written it together as rapidly and as satisfyingly as we did.

THE AUTHORS' WORK
IN ORGANIZATIONS

Roger Evans and Peter Russell work together on a variety of consulting and training projects in different parts of the world, using the ideas and principles of creative management outlined in these pages. In addition they each have their own consulting and training practices.

ROGER EVANS is interested in developing long-term relations with organizations who want to understand the 'hard' human skills of the 1990s, and who recognize the need to create a learning environment for these skills and to empower their people. He is Managing Director of Creative Learning Consultants, a consulting and educational group. This group has developed its activities on a broad front, working extensively with business corporations and also in the field of government and social policy. In all these areas, CLC uses a new learning methodology that puts into practice the material in this book. It also has a training programme in this process for professionals.

Creative Learning Consultants
The Barn
Nan Clarks Lane
London NW7 4HH
England

PETER RUSSELL works with a number of corporations who are seeking new ways to manage the future. Much of this work focuses on the role which self-management plays in the development of individuals, organizations and society as a whole. He is particularly interested in the long-term implications of social and technological innovation, and the changes in human thinking that these could bring. He believes that only by exploring and developing our inner potential can we meet the challenges of the twenty-first century. As well as speaking on this subject to various organizations and institutions, he runs various programmes in the related areas of stress management, mindsets, the learning process and creative thinking, and facilitates sessions on creative problem-solving and brainstorming.

Peter Russell
BM Noetics
London WC1N 3XX
England

FURTHER READING

The following are some of the books mentioned in the text that we have found very useful in our own work and development. We give details here for those who wish to explore some of these areas more deeply.

Adams, James L., *Conceptual Blockbusting: A Pleasurable Guide to Better Problem Solving* (Norton, London 1978).

Beer, Stafford, *Platform for Change* (John Wiley, Chichester, 1975).

Belbin, R. Meredith, *Management Teams: Why They Succeed or Fail* (Heinemann, London, 1981).

Brown, Mark, *The Dinosaur Strain: The Survivor's Guide to Personal and Business Success* (Element, Shaftesbury, 1988).

Emerson, Ralph Waldo, 'Self Reliance' in *The Complete Works of Ralph Waldo Emerson,* ed. Edward W. Emerson, 1903-4.

Ferguson, Marilyn, *The Aquarian Conspiracy: Personal and Social Transformation in the 1980s* (Routledge and Kegan Paul, London, 1982).

Fisher, Roger and Brown, Scott, *Getting Together: Building a Relationship that Gets to Yes* (Houghton Mifflin, Boston, 1988).

Fisher Roger and Ury, William, *Getting to Yes: Negotiating for Agreement Without Giving In* (Houghton Mifflin, Boston, 1981).

Fulghum, Robert, *Everything I Need to Know I Learned in Kindergarten* (Villard, New York, 1989).

Goldberg, Philip, *The Intuitive Edge: Understanding and Developing Intuition* (Tarcher, Los Angeles, 1983).

Harvey-Jones, John, *Making It Happen: Reflections on Leadership* (Collins, London, 1988).

Kelly, Marjorie, 'Revolution in the Marketplace' *Utne Reader*, Jan/Feb 1989.

Kilmann, Ralph H., *Beyond the Quick Fix: Managing Five Tracks to Organizational Success* (Jossey-Bass, London, 1986).

Kinsman, Francis, *The New Agenda* (Spencer Stuart, London, 1983).

Lynch, James J., *The Language of the Heart: The Body's Response to Human Dialogue* (Basic Books, New York, 1985).

MacNulty, Chris, *The Future of the UK 2010* (Applied Futures Ltd report, London, February 1989).

MacNulty, W. Kirk , 'UK Social Change Through a Wide-Angle Lens' *Futures*, August 1985.

Morgan, Gareth, *Images of Organization* (Sage Publications, London, 1986).

Morgan, Gareth, *Riding the Waves of Change: Developing Managerial Competencies for a Turbulent World* (Jossey-Bass, London, 1988).

Naisbitt, John, *Megatrends: Ten New Directions Transforming our Lives* (Warner, New York, 1982).

Naisbitt, John and Aburdene, Patricia, *Re-Inventing the Corporation* (Warner, New York, 1985).

Nixon, Peter G. F., 'Stress and the Cardiovascular System' *Practioner*, September 1982, 226, 1589-98.

Peters, Tom, *Thriving on Chaos : Handbook for a Management Revolution* (Macmillan, London, 1987).

Ray, Michael and Myers, Rochelle, *Creativity in Business* (Doubleday, New York, 1986).

Schofield, Robert E., *The Lunar Society of Birmingham: A Social History of Provincial Science and Industry in Eighteenth-Century England* (Clarendon Press, Oxford, 1963).

Schwartz, Tony, 'Acceleration Syndrome: Does Everyone Live in the Fast Lane Nowadays' *Vanity Fair*, October 1988.

Scully, John, with Byrne, John A., *Odyssey* (Harper & Row, New York, 1987).